I0168615

THE NEW MASON'S BOOK

BY

MICHAEL R. POLL

The New Mason's Book
By Michael R. Poll

A Cornerstone Book
Published by Cornerstone Book Publishers
Copyright © 2025 by Cornerstone Book Publishers

All rights reserved under International and Pan-American Copyright Conventions. No part of this book may be reproduced in any manner without permission in writing from the copyright holder, except by a reviewer, who may quote brief passages in a review.

Cornerstone Book Publishers
Hot Springs Village, AR

First Cornerstone Edition – 2025

www.cornerstonepublishers.com

ISBN: 978-1-61342-457-5

Table of Contents

INTRODUCTION

The period immediately before and after receiving the Blue Lodge degrees is critical. These degrees, which are the Entered Apprentice, Fellow Craft, and Master Mason degrees, are the foundation of Freemasonry. Information not provided during this time can pose problems for new Masons. Please allow me to share some thoughts with you.

This book is designed for both the new Mason and the petitioner seeking to join Masonry (since both can be considered 'new'). While nothing contained in this work is of a secret nature, some may be best appreciated after one has received the third degree. As such, some initial thought was given to doing this as several separate books — before joining and after each degree. But this seemed cumbersome and since most anything any candidate seeks can be found online (but with questionable value), I felt that doing this as a stand-alone book may best serve everyone. If you have yet to complete all of the Masonic degrees of the craft lodge, please read this as a guidebook in preparing your mind for future initiations and experiences.

If you have completed some or all of the craft lodge degrees, use the information provided to reinforce or augment your understanding of Masonry and pass on that knowledge to others who have yet to fully experience the initiations.

I'd like to first say a few words to the candidates looking to join Freemasonry. What you have done and are doing will lead you to a larger world. But no, if you have read that joining Freemasonry will give you the powers of a Jedi or that you will share in the secret wealth of the world, you fell for some nonsense. Freemasonry will provide you with none of that. At least, Freemasonry will give you none of that if you understand *wealth* to mean money. But if you truly study the teachings of Freemasonry, you can receive wealth far more important to the wise individual. Freemasonry can give you the keys to unlocking parts within you that can lead you to a spiritually rich, better life. By putting the teachings of Freemasonry into practice, you can become a better human being. The Masonic rituals and teachings can unlock doors for you, all designed to help you become better than you are today. But unlocked doors will mean nothing unless you take the steps necessary to walk into the room.

If you are someone who has yet to receive their first degree, there are a few things I'd like to talk to you about. If you're waiting for your initiation, this means that you have been balloted upon and you have passed the ballot. All the members of your future lodge who were present voted on you and desire you to be a part of their lodge — their family. Masons call each other "brothers," and we do so because we are considered family. But it's the act of balloting that I'd like to speak about for a moment. Freemasonry is often said to be tied to the Ancient Mystery Schools through initiation. Initiation in Freemasonry is a symbolic journey of self-discovery and personal growth. The craft lodge will provide you with three initiations, which can be looked upon as the keys to opening those doors that I just spoke about. There is an old thought about initiation that I would like to pass on. The idea is that for initiation to be considered valid, three elements must be present. One is the desire to *be initiated*, the second is the desire *to initiate*, and the third is the *proper setting*. The desire for your being initiated was satisfied when you submitted your petition. Freemasonry insists that no one should be talked into joining

Masonry, but they must come of their own free will. For initiation to be valid, there must be a clear desire to be initiated. The desire to initiate was satisfied with your ballot.

The third element of the successful initiation comprises several key parts. The proper setting is the lodge room, or in other organizations that initiate, whatever room is designated as the initiation room. During an initiation, there should be no horse-play, laughter, joking around, or anything else that can take away from the solemn event that is taking place. All present, including you — the candidate — should have an open and clear mind. Should anyone in the lodge, through carelessness or ignorance, break the solemn mood of the initiation, dismiss them and ignore them. You can control no one else, but you can control yourself. No one is there to make fun of you, use you as a source of entertainment, harass you, or do anything other than offer you the opportunity, through initiation, to open the door to a possibly more rewarding life. It is enough for you to know that initiation is far older than Freemasonry and older than most societies. By having a peaceful mind, being as aware as possible, and staying open to your feelings, you increase the chances of the initiation being a deeply moving memory that you will carry with you all your life.

As for technical points, I suggest that you find out the type of lodge that you are joining before your first initiation. When I mention the 'type' of lodge, I'm referring to whether it is a more formal or casual setting. Some lodges place a greater emphasis on ritual and education regarding the various aspects of Masonic symbolism than others. These types of lodges usually dress in dark or business suits. If you are unsure, ask ahead of time how you should dress for your initiation. Showing that you care about details may mean a lot.

After your first initiation, you will usually be assigned to an instructor to learn the ritual work expected by your jurisdiction. This instructor will guide you in understanding the rituals and teachings of Freemasonry. But this is something that can vary depending on the jurisdiction. In some jurisdictions, new initiates are assigned to a class of instruction. In such classes, students may be assigned instructors on a lasting or temporary basis. Whatever the practice is for your jurisdiction, do the work. It is neither a waste of your time nor unnecessary busy work. There is an old thought that whatever comes your way free and easy is worth what you paid for it. In the old schools of initiation, payment was *always* necessary for anything one received by means of initiation. Payment may not have been made in actual money, but work was required. It made the initiate realize that what they were receiving was of value. Consider setting aside at least a few hours a week for your Masonic study. Meet with your instructor, or instructors, as often as possible. Listen to them, do what they ask, and in the very beginning, try to temper any possible enthusiasm you have and limit your questions and actions to what is asked of you. There will come a time and place for all of your questions.

The actual examination of the candidates and what is expected of them varies from jurisdiction to jurisdiction. If you are sincere in joining Masonry, do what is asked of you. Spend the time necessary to learn the work. If situations in your life unexpectedly change and you simply cannot make the time to do the work required to advance, make this change in your situation known to your instructors. Most jurisdictions have time limits on completing your work. However, if the situation changes for a candidate, making it impossible for them to learn their work and advance in the degrees in the time necessary, this will rarely be held against the candidate. Your family and work come before the lodge and should be given first consideration. Time for Masonry may come at a later date.

I believe it's best that while one is an Entered Apprentice, or Fellowcraft, they should hold most of the questions about Freemasonry, save aspects of their degrees needed for advancement, and keep general information about the history and philosophy of

Freemasonry on hold until their work is complete. I believe that their total focus should be on the work given to them. But once a candidate receives the Master Mason degree, no question about the Blue Lodge should be held back. If answers to questions cannot be found in your lodge, seek them elsewhere. The goal of a new Master Mason is to learn as much as possible about the craft, its reason for existing, its practices, as well as its history and philosophy. But a warning, be careful with the internet. So much out there is just outright wrong. In addition, if you ask questions about pretty much anything concerning your lodge on the internet, you may get answers back from very experienced Masons who will be giving you answers that may be perfectly correct for their jurisdiction, but completely wrong for yours.

I also suggest paying close attention to the workings of your lodge. If your jurisdiction has been wise enough to change back the alterations of the early to mid-1800s, restricting lodge business to only Master Masons, and your jurisdiction has gone back to the original practice of allowing Entered Apprentices in your business meetings, then your study of lodge operation should have begun earlier. Watch carefully how business is done in the lodge. Watch the actions of each of the officers, how they conduct themselves, and interact with the membership. Visit the lodges in your jurisdiction, preferably in your own area. Learn the meeting dates of the lodges near you. Attend whenever possible. Read as much as you can on Freemasonry. An encyclopedia or dictionary of Freemasonry is always helpful. *Mackey's Encyclopedia of Freemasonry* is considered a classic. The original editions are long out of print but can often be found in used bookstores. Reprints can easily be found.[1] Research societies and lodges are highly recommended. Many jurisdictions have state research lodges that can provide much useful information in the United States. Also, do not, Do Not forget to study well your lodge By-Laws!

There is a danger, however, if you are a new Mason and you happen to have joined a lodge that is struggling with membership.

The danger is that new Masons will often be grabbed and put into leadership positions before they even know exactly what goes into opening or closing a lodge. Be careful of that and do not be afraid to say no. I believe it is far better to wait a while and take office after a few years of seasoning.

Also, be careful of those who seek titles. We are not Freemasons to gain power, status, or glory. We are Freemasons to gain enlightenment and learn how to better live in this world with our fellow human beings. Power seekers or brokers have no place in Masonry, and if or when you encounter them, have nothing to do with them.

This is one thing that you should always remember: we represent Freemasonry to the world. Our actions, good or bad, will be how Freemasonry itself is viewed. Do not go out in the world and disrespect either yourself or Freemasonry. Your conduct outside of the lodge, especially in public, is to be of a nature that will be a credit to Masonry and not a disgrace.

Michael R. Poll

Notes

1. Mackey, Albert. *Mackey's Encyclopedia of Freemasonry*. New Orleans, LA: Cornerstone Book Publishers. Reprint, 2015.

THE NEW MASON'S BOOK

Symbolism

I'd like to explore a few aspects of the Craft Degrees in Freemasonry. The idea is to examine how and why we do certain things — and how things may have changed from the very early days of the Operative Freemasons.

Today's craft lodge has three degrees — the Entered Apprentice, Fellowcraft, and Master Mason. These degrees, born out of the inspiration of the old Operative Freemasons, the builders of the great cathedrals of the Middle Ages, have transformed over time, yet still carry the essence of their origins.

In the days of the old Operative Masons, a young boy who showed promise and who was found to be honest and worthy was taken in by a Master craftsman and would serve about seven years as an apprentice. He was essentially a helper and would learn all aspects of the building trade taught to him by his Master.

When the Master felt that his apprentice had learned all that he could be taught, and his work was judged to be acceptable, he would be given something of a test.

The apprentice would be asked to complete a "Master-piece." This would be some piece of work that would represent the skill and ability of the apprentice. If he passed this trial, he would be accepted into the guild as a *Fellow of the Craft*. This meant that he was a full member of the guild and able to earn wages like any other member.

The idea of degrees in Masonry may not have existed in the time of the old Operatives. In the early Manuscripts of Operative Masonry, we see only mention of *Apprentices, Fellows,* and *lodge officers*. The degrees seem to have been developed in the 1700s. The lodges formed themselves and evolved into what we have today as a three-degree craft lodge system.

When we look at our degrees today, they can be confusing and often open to misinterpretation. Things that we do, things that we expect of the candidates, and even many of the words that we use can be … problematic. They seem to be of a different time. That's because it's true. They *are* of a different time. Many of our words and practices date back hundreds of years. Let's examine some of our practices and their potential meanings.

Freemasonry presents many of its lessons by means of symbolism. A symbol is simply one thing that is used to represent something else. A sign on a building with a piano can be used to quickly show that this is a music store that sells pianos. In the early days of Operative Freemasonry, most people couldn't read. An inn might have an image of a mug of ale, or a bed, or something else helpful, rather than relying only on spelling out the word *inn*.

The symbols we use in Freemasonry, rooted in the work of the old Operatives, carry profound moral meanings. They represent various aspects of Operative Freemasonry, but we can also assign to them additional meanings related to morality, human character development, and goodwill. This emphasis on moral development and social contribution is at the heart of Freemasonry, inspiring us to be better members of society.

Let's talk now about one of the most misunderstood and questioned aspects of Freemasonry — the Obligation. What does it mean, and why do we need it?

But first, we need to recognize something. For nearly as long as Speculative Freemasonry has existed, there have been anti-Masons. Freemasonry is one of the most attractive targets for conspiracy theories. Anti-Masons love to claim that we seek to take over the world, possess vast riches, and guard over all the world's wealth by means of terrible *blood oaths* that we extract from unsuspecting candidates.

I really don't know how many times I have sat around a dinner table at lodges with Masons who were laughing about such nonsense. "Where's *my* share?" "Why did they leave *me* out of all the riches??" It is nonsense born out of ignorance of Freemasonry and a failure to think out the situation. But some do choose to believe in unicorns.

Operative Freemasonry worked under strict rules and laws. Guilds, fraternities, and other such organizations had more or less standard forms of oaths or obligations which were approved by both the crown and the Church. They were basically, "do this" and "don't do that." The actual penalties for violating any of the obligations of the Operatives were the same then as they are today in Speculative Freemasonry. The actual penalties consisted of reprimand, fines, suspension, or expulsion. That's it. They were and are few and simple. Any actual capital penalties then or now would violate civil and religious laws.

In the Middle Ages, lodges of Operative Freemasons existed at the will and pleasure of both the crown and the Church. If these lodges (or later, Speculative ones) had included any obligations in their charter that violated the law or rules and acted on them, they would have been disbanded and arrested.

But symbolism has always played a part in all aspects of Freemasonry. We also must remember that to be just expelled from a lodge of Operative Freemasons in the Middle Ages could have meant an actual death sentence to an Operative Mason. Working was how they put food on the table for themselves and their family. They needed to work to live. To be expelled means they could no longer feed themselves or their family. They would also be excluded from the group's physical protection and would face the dangers of the harsh and often cruel Medieval world alone. It was a dangerous and harsh time. Today, expulsion from Freemasonry means only that you can no longer enjoy being a Freemason. Life was different in the Middle Ages.

One of the most recognized symbols of Freemasonry is the Square and Compasses. These were implements used by Operative Freemasons, and in Freemasonry, they symbolize morality and the importance of living a balanced life. The Masonic apron, another well-recognized symbol, is more than just a protective garment. It is a badge of innocence and a reminder for Masons to live by a moral code of conduct.

The white leather apron, while today being mostly white cloth aprons, is said to be an emblem of innocence and the badge of a Mason. This means that Masons are taught to live by a moral code of conduct. Masons who refuse to live within our moral code or who violate the laws of their community can be expelled.

The Masonic apron also denotes Masonic rank and office, not only within the lodge, but also within the district or Grand Lodge.

Speculative Freemasons today, by far, do not work in the actual building trade. Some may be actual stone masons by profession, but it is certainly not required. In our lodges, we don't use the Working Tools of Freemasons as they were initially intended. For example, the 24-inch gauge was another Operative working tool, but for us today, it is a symbol of proper time management. It teaches us to recognize the need to use our time on Earth to serve the Almighty, help our fellow man, and do so in ways that help us grow into better human beings.

The common gavel was an actual working tool and is a symbol for us to chip off the rough edges in our character and moral development. On our altars is the Holy Bible, which is the rule and guide to our faith and practices. Many of our lessons and teachings come directly from the Bible. While our doors are open to worthy men from all faiths and practices, we draw the teachings for our candidates from the symbolic lessons within the Bible.

The Square is also one of the actual working tools of the Operatives. But in our Speculative Masonry, it is one of our many symbols from which we teach moral lessons. The Square is also the insignia of the office of Worshipful Master. In addition, it has also worked its way into our common language. We speak of a "square deal" with the meaning that it was a fair or honest deal. Other Masonic symbols, words, and practices have also worked themselves into our culture and language.

If you are a new Mason, or one who has, or is, thinking about petitioning, or even an experienced Mason, please listen for a minute. The goal of the old Operatives when taking in an apprentice was simple. They wanted to teach him all that they knew so that he would become a highly skilled worker who would bring honor, respect, and work to their guild. Our goal as Speculative Freemasons is to take in candidates and, by means of moral, symbolic lessons, have them become better human beings and more valued members of society.

It is strongly suggested that you study your Masonic Monitor, Law Book, and other educational materials available from your Grand Lodge and other sources thoroughly. Unlike those who did not learn their work in the days of the Operatives, no one will expel you from Speculative Freemasonry for failing to learn our advanced symbolic lessons. The only required work (in many jurisdictions) is the memorization of certain catechisms to advance to the Fellowcraft and then Master Mason degrees. Beyond that, nothing is required to be learned.

But if you spend time and learn all that is offered in the Entered Apprentice degree, as well as those that follow, you will have a more enlightened and rewarding life. Freemasonry will not force anything on you. But you do not become "better" by only joining, paying your dues, and doing the minimal that is expected from you. It takes serious work, dedication, and a desire to improve yourself.

Freemasonry can open the door for you, but you will be the one required to decide if you walk in or stay on the outside.

THE BLUE LODGE

L et's delve today into an intriguing question that often sparks curiosity among Freemasons — why are our craft lodges called "Blue Lodges"? This question looks at into the abstract nature of our symbolic teachings, and requires a bit of personal interpretation. It's a puzzle with no definitive answer, but rather a matter of opinion based on a general understanding of symbolism.

The most commonly cited answer, as far as I've encountered, is that our lodges are called Blue Lodges because the sky is blue. This explanation, rooted in the idea that the old Operative lodges often convened outside on hilltops, seems to provide a simple solution. However, if we study this answer, it also raises some intriguing questions and potential problems.

You see, the old Operatives were a labor organization. They worked during the day, and their lodges would meet for business after their work was completed. But, when would that be, at night or on the weekend? Some Masonic historians suggest that lodges would meet on those hilltops for their business meetings on Saturday afternoons. This would give them a blue sky above them. But are we sure about that? Are we so sure that the old Operatives had a five-day work week? I'm not convinced.

The Church controlled many aspects of medieval life, including work. Work on Sunday was not allowed. It was a day for rest and religion. This would seem to mean that there were no business meetings of lodges on Sundays. But what about Saturdays?

The usual eight-hour-a-day, five-days-a-week working schedule is a modern invention. It seems far more logical that the old Operatives' work schedule was from sunup to sundown. They would work as many days of the week (Sundays excluded) that were necessary to complete their contracted job.

A nine-to-five workday does not seem practical for them, as, for example, their days would be much shorter in the winter months. Daylight was necessary as they had no floodlights to see to do their work. They worked when the sun came up and until it went down. The sun was their clock.

So, if they held their business meetings on these hilltops at night, it would not be a blue sky. Perhaps the answer lies in their appreciation for the day's blue sky? Maybe. But maybe there is more to the answer.

Blue, the color of the sky and the sea, holds a multitude of symbolic meanings. It represents heaven, wisdom, trust, loyalty, intelligence, confidence, faith, truth, and even the Word of God. This rich tapestry of interpretations adds depth to our understanding of the color blue.

I've read of tests conducted with this color showing a slowing down of human metabolism, and just looking at the color can produce a calming effect. Dark blue, or purple, is also considered a royal color and symbolizes purity and sincerity.

In advertising, blue is often used to promote products and services related to cleanliness or cleaning products. Blue is also associated with airliners, airports, and air conditioning companies, suggesting an association with the sky, clean, cool air, or comfort.

We use blue for services or companies relating to the sea or water, such as cruise ships, or even some bottled water companies. Blue is also often used to suggest precision when promoting high-tech products. Blue is commonly viewed in modern society (but not always) as a masculine color; hence, another reason that male Freemasonry may have adopted the color blue in its early days.

Light blue is often associated with health, healing, tranquility, understanding, and softness. Dark blue usually represents knowledge, power, integrity, and seriousness.

I believe that we would be hard-pressed to provide only one answer as to why Freemasonry associates blue with its lodges. But the most valuable symbols are those with multiple meanings or ways to speak to us. Any valuable symbol, by its nature, must be understood or able to be interpreted by more than one meaning.

In the early days, teaching by symbols was a means to provide information to students in an environment where some teachings were forbidden. A symbol might have a completely innocent interpretation to satisfy the authorities while still being able to provide deeper meanings to initiates. A symbol would provide both teachings and protection from those who did not desire such teachings to take place.

Such is the nature of a symbol and one of the reasons why Freemasonry finds such value in this form of ancient teachings. While we do not fear authorities forbidding our teachings, we do have varying levels of understanding among our members. Some may wish only the superficial teachings of our Order, while others might want to explore its deeper aspects. Our symbols can be explored to discover their deeper meanings, or they can be appreciated from a superficial viewpoint, understanding only their total meaning. The choice is always ours.

By the way, I see blue as refreshing, pure, and inviting. That's my personal interpretation of why blue is used in "Blue Lodge." I may be dead wrong, but it feels good to me.

The Apprentice and the Masterpiece

In the days of the old Operative Masons, becoming a Freemason was hard, difficult work. The Apprentice needed to show proficiency with his working tools, a willingness to work hard, and to possess an outstanding character. He needed to prove that he had the heart of a Freemason, be of lawful age (and that would be whatever age they determined), be sincere in his desire to learn, and be found worthy by use of an entire collection of demands required for membership. Also, he had to often bind himself to serve under strict rules for up to seven years. The quality of his work during the time of his service was, in itself, a test of his character and ability. If he was found to be incompetent or unworthy, he was sent home.

During the Middle Ages, Apprentices in the Operative Guilds were not only taught the art of building, but also seem to have engaged in a comprehensive study of the liberal arts and sciences (most likely done during times they were not working). This approach aimed to produce fully rounded Master Masons. Any perceived lack of ability, failure to follow instructions, or questions about character could abruptly end an Apprentice's career.

During the early years, the Apprentice was given the most lowly of tasks and was, in reality, little more than a servant to the Masters and Fellows of the Craft. If he proved himself competent and responsible, his wages could be increased. This would also allow his work and study to continue.

As per the Old Charges, an Apprentice was expected to live under numerous restrictions and maintain a sterling moral reputation and work ethic. These strict standards were a testament to the importance of character in Freemasonry.

An apprenticeship might also end for offences such as being absent without permission, failure to be respectful to Masters or Fellows of the Craft, slander, or even an evening at a tavern. Certainly, an Apprentice turning up drunk or with a hangover would end his association with the craft.

Their work was demanding, and their lives were highly structured and restricted. The only hope of success lay in diligent and proficient work, continually making personal advancements and adhering to the many rules. After seven years of study & service, and *if* he was found worthy, he was invited to submit his "Master Piece." This was not just a piece of stone or metal, but a representation of his transformation into a skilled Freemason. It was his final exam, marking the end of his apprenticeship and the beginning of a new chapter in his life.

The submitted work was carefully inspected by the Master, and if it was found acceptable, he was declared a Master. He could then be entitled to accept his tools and travel with the other Fellows on job assignments. But the Masterpiece may not have been the end-all for the new Master. Continuing research on the old Operatives provides some interesting information.

Today, the degree structure of the craft lodge is Entered Apprentice, Fellowcraft, and Master Mason. But that structure may not accurately reflect the original design of the Operatives. In its earliest days, Speculative Freemasonry had only two degrees. The Master Mason degree was added later. But, while it seems that

Speculative Freemasonry built upon the model of the old Operatives, there were some changes.

There is no evidence that I have seen to suggest that the old Operatives had a degree structure. They were basically working or not. It was a building trade. It was how they made their living. Today, we view an Entered Apprentice as someone new to Masonry. This *does* match up with the Apprentices of the old Operatives. But how do the Fellowcraft and Master Mason degrees match with the system of the old Operatives? Well, they really don't. In fact, it seems that in the old Operative guilds, one was a Master[1] before he was a *Fellow of the Craft*. This may be because these distinctions would have been in relation to their accomplishments and status within a guild.

Let's think of an Apprentice as someone who is in college. They are learning. At some point, they must take their final exam, and if they pass, they will receive their diploma and be entitled to be called a graduate. This is similar to when the Apprentice would complete his studies and submit his Masterpiece. If it were accepted, he would become a Master. He had graduated from his Apprenticeship. However, a new college graduate does not receive a salary solely for being a graduate. He needs to find a job in order to earn a salary.

A Master in the old Operatives had proven his skill and value, but he did not start drawing a salary until he was accepted into a guild as a Fellow of the Craft. In other words, he earned money from the moment he was hired. That's when he would start drawing his pay. A Master had not just proven his worth, but he had also achieved a significant milestone. He had graduated from his Apprenticeship. Being a Master allowed him to become acceptable for hire, or a Fellow of the Craft. Being a Fellow of the Craft was a title that filled him with pride and a sense of accomplishment. He was worthy of hire and working with the other Fellows.

So, with that understanding, the top dog was the one who was not only a Master but also earning a living. Of course, in our

Speculative Lodges, we have rituals for each of our craft degrees. But the question must be asked, "Were rituals of any sort used by the old operatives?" The answer is a very definite, "I'm not sure."

Certainly, rituals have been around since the dawn of man, and some have been associated with the Operatives. We have records of various ceremonies and initiations for anything that was felt to be important or significant. Submitting a Masterpiece after many years of hard work would certainly seem to qualify as an important event. In addition, teaching by means of symbols is also an ancient form of education.

That Speculative Freemasonry employs symbols in its education and ceremonies is not by chance. That we have initiations is also not by chance. I believe that the old Operatives taught many of their advanced lessons using symbols and employed ceremonies, rituals, and initiations for their new Masters. I believe that when the Fellows of the Craft were not engaged in labor on a cathedral or other building projects, they used their time to advance themselves through education, ceremonies, and initiations. They were not just building cathedrals but building the self.

There is another aspect of the Masterpiece we need to consider. An Apprentice worked for many years to achieve his goal of being a Fellow of the Craft. It was hard, many times menial work, and he could have failed at any point. There were no guarantees of success. This was not a case of someone just showing up and being given positions or considerations simply because they were there. It was necessary that he prove his worth time and again. There was no guarantee that even if he were allowed to work all the way up to submitting his Masterpiece, it would be accepted. Certainly, many were not. There is a lesson here.

We value what we work hard to achieve. What comes to us easily is often of little value. The Masterpiece can represent the work or price that we must pay for anything in Masonry that we may receive. It's not about money; it's about the work we put into something. If we believe that fees or dues are the price expected to be paid, then we have missed one of the most important of Masonic lessons. If we believe that we are due anything simply because we show up, or that there is no need to learn the work because others did not, we are wrong. Anyone who believes such things has no real understanding of Freemasonry.

The work is necessary to sort the worthy ones from the unworthy. We don't build buildings. We build the self, and the way we prove our worth is by living what we teach.

Notes

1. By the word *Master,* I am speaking of a level of achievement, not the one in charge of a lodge of Masons.

THE 24-INCH GAUGE

I'd like to look at one of the symbolic working tools of Freemasonry. It's one that we learn about as Entered Apprentice Masons. To start with, I'd like to give you an excerpt from *The Louisiana Monitor*. If you're from another jurisdiction, this short section may vary slightly in the wording, but the meaning will be the same.

> "The 24-inch gauge is an implement used by the Operative Masons to measure and lay out their work; but we, as Free and Accepted Masons, or taught to use it for the more noble and glorious purpose of dividing our time. It being divided into 24 equal parts, is emblematic of the 24 hours of the day, which we are taught to divide into three equal parts; whereby are found eight hours for the service of God and a distressed, worthy brother, eight for our usual vocations, and eight for refreshment and sleep."[1]

So, let's stop for a minute and think about what's being said here. If we break it down, then we can see that the 24-inch gauge is a symbol for time management. We use it to remind us of how to best spend our time each day. But is this division of time workable today?

We are told that the 24-hour day should be divided into three parts: eight hours for the service of God or a distressed Mason, eight hours for work, and eight hours for sleep or other activities. What about our family? Where do they fit in? What if we were required by economics to work more than eight hours a day? Is this a realistic division of our time?

The lesson of the 24-inch gauge is symbolic. It's not a rigid set of instructions, but a tool that empowers us to manage our time effectively. A symbol holds value for us because it can teach us something that may not be immediately obvious. The lesson being taught here is one of balance.

I don't believe that we should serve God with a stopwatch in our hand. I can't imagine punching a time clock and ending God's work when our time is up. I don't believe that's what's meant here. The point is that we should balance our day with everything vital to us as humans.

We need to take action to provide for ourselves and our families. We need to make time for our family, rest, eat, sleep, and relax. We must do the work that the Almighty has put us here to do, which includes helping others as well as ourselves. If we do any one of these things to the exclusion of all else, then we become out of balance.

Once we are out of balance, we're not able to properly do any of the tasks needed for a successful life. The lesson of the 24-inch gauge is to teach us to stop and look at the entire picture of our life.

We should spend our days doing what the Almighty intended: enjoying life and recognizing that we are only part of the whole. We should live our lives in a way that ensures we will be remembered as someone worthy when we are gone.

There is an old saying, "all work and no play makes Jack a dull boy." It's true. If all we do is try to earn money or do anything to excess, then we become out of balance. Our life will not be rounded and complete.

The lesson of the 24-inch gauge is not meant to teach us to watch the clock and be rigid as to how we spend our time. It teaches us that we should be well-rounded and do everything necessary for a productive and valuable life. It's a guiding principle that reassures us that balance is key to a fulfilling life.

Notes

1. Huckaby, G.C., Compiler, *The Louisiana Monitor,* 1988, p. 31.

THE COMMON GAVEL

This paper delves into another of the symbolic working tools of Freemasonry—the Common Gavel, which represents the journey of self-improvement.

First, it's important to clarify that the Common Gavel we're discussing in this paper is *distinct from* the gavels used by the Worshipful Master and the two Wardens. These gavels serve a different purpose, primarily used for instruction or information during meetings or degrees. The Common Gavel, on the other hand, is a symbol of self-improvement that can be used by individual Masons or the entire lodge.

The Common Gavel we're discussing here is not just a tool, but a symbol with a unique interpretation in Speculative Masonry. Each Mason uses it for specific reasons, as outlined in *The Louisiana Monitor*. While this interpretation may vary slightly in other jurisdictions, the core meaning remains the same.

"The common gavel is an implement used by Operative Masons to break off the corners of rough stones, the better to fit them for the builder's use. But we, as Free and Accepted Masons, are taught to use it for the more noble and glorious purpose of divesting our hearts and consciousness of all the vices and superficialities of life; thereby fitting our minds as living stones for that spiritual build-ing, that house not made with hands, eternal in the heavens."[1]

As with many of the symbols in Freemasonry, we have taken something with an ordinary meaning and applied new meanings that may not be obvious to the casual observer. One of these new meanings is the importance of humility in effective leadership. This should make us all the more respectful and appreciative of leaders who embody this quality.

We can think of our use of the common gavel as more of an action than an actual working tool. The common gavel can be seen as an act of self-improvement. The symbolic stone that is being worked on in Speculative Masonry is known as the rough ashlar. For an Operative Mason, the rough ashlar is a stone arriving directly from the quarry. At the quarry, they would quickly cut out a piece of rough stone and send it to the worksite. Then at the worksite, stone masons would smooth out the stones using their gavels. The stones would then be in a useful condition to be placed directly into whatever they were building.

In Speculative Masonry, we interpret the rough ashlar as an individual human being. He is of sound material but needs work. He's "rough around the edges," untrained, and untaught. He is said to be in darkness.

The common gavel is the act of smoothing out those rough edges or teaching him, bringing him to Light. In Freemasonry, 'Light' symbolizes knowledge, understanding, and spiritual en-lightenment. The common gavel smooths out a rough ashlar for the Operative Mason and turns it into what is known as a *Perfect Ashlar,* or something useful for their work.

The goal of the lessons in Speculative Masonry is to take the sound, but rough and untrained human being, knock off all the rough edges, and make him of such quality that he can live a more rewarding, spiritual life. He becomes a living Perfect Ashlar. He is useful to humanity.

If we think of an Operative Lodge, we can imagine rows of Operative Masons working on rough pieces of stone. They are all doing the same thing. They're trying to improve their stones beyond their original state. They are doing the best possible work given their skills.

In Speculative Freemasonry, we might think of the Operative Lodge as the entire Earth. The rough stone or ashlar is our life. Everyone is trying to do the same thing: make their life better. But not everyone will end up improving. Not everyone has the right tools or instruction. Not everyone is interested in doing the work needed for self-improvement. But for those willing to do the work, the common gavel can be seen as that act that makes the good person better. This is a lifelong task. It's a task that ends only with the end of our physical lives. The responsibility for this task lies solely with each individual, empowering them to take control of their own self-improvement journey.

The state of an ashlar at the close of anyone's physical life will depend on the work that they have done during their life. Of course, there are also rules regarding how we use our common gavels.

We might envision a large classroom or an old Operative Lodge, where many people work together on their own personal rough stones. We can see the people around us doing their work, and we can see their progress. It's not considered cheating to observe someone doing exceptional work and try to emulate their technique in our own work. It's also not considered cheating if someone sees what we are doing and tries to copy our work. This is considered working together and simply trying to lift each other up by example.

What is considered cheating is to directly involve ourselves in another's work. It's not allowed for you to chip away at another's stone any more than someone should be allowed to chip away at yours. We all do our own work.

There is a significant difference between viewing another's work, recognizing the skill present in it, and deciding for yourself that you want to work at that level of skill, rather than doing the actual work for someone else. There is no personal advancement in having your work accomplished by someone else. For example, let's say that your friend's neighbor is ill, but needs some work done around his house. Going to your friend's house and helping out his neighbor secretly, allowing the neighbor to think your friend was the helper, does not help your friend be a better person. We all must do our own work.

There is another aspect of self-improvement that I must cover. And it's not a very pleasant one. It has to do with envy. It's when we look at someone else's work and recognize its skill and quality, but instead of trying to emulate that work in our own, we become envious. We do nothing but stare in anger at the beautiful work of another. We allow the negative aspects of human nature to take control of us. We may feel envy, jealousy, and then bitterness and resentment. "Why can't *I* be doing work like *him*?" Or, "Why should *they* be able to do what *I* can't do?" If ego controls us or guides our work, then destruction can follow. There will be no self-improvement at all.

Negative feelings not only hinder our personal growth but also create unproductive obstacles for others. From an organizational standpoint, if our leaders are controlled by ego and lust for power or glory, then the only ones they will select as their lieutenants (the ones who will follow them) will be those of evident lesser skill. Ego and envy will cause such leaders to hold back, deny advancement, or destroy the reputation of anyone whom they believe could possibly outshine them. The quality of leadership will then diminish with each subsequent change, ultimately rendering the organization of no value.

All of our leaders must be of the highest skill and moral quality. They must recognize that we all shine with our own level and variety of light. A leader *must not* be envious of the skill of another but rejoice when he finds great skill in the work of another. Great skill in a subordinate means the future success of the whole organization. The organization's long-term success should always be the goal of the true leader. Make no mistake, the ego must never be allowed to take control. The ego can destroy all that we hold dear.

In any work towards self-improvement, we should recognize that generosity of spirit, kindness, and peace of mind are key to any successful life. But we must also acknowledge the need for unyielding determination to prevent the unworthy from gaining access or remaining in any sort of leadership position. A useful life must be of benefit to us and others. We must showcase the good work of others. We must recognize and acknowledge the good work of others and find ways to incorporate it into our own work. The work may be rewarding, but it will also be challenging at times.

When someone asks for help, we should be generous without doing their work for them or forcing changes they don't want. We must recognize that we all have our own paths. No one has the right to force an unwanted path on anyone else. And when our days are done, we must be ready to display our work for examination. Of course, the catch is that since we never know when that day will come, wasting time or putting off until *later,* our work on personal advancements could be a serious mistake. Do your work now. Tomorrow may never come.

Notes

1. Huckaby, G.C., Compiler, *The Louisiana Monitor,* 1988, p. 32.

Hiram Abif

A round the world, there are many different types of Freemasonry. By that, I mean the rituals that are used and practiced. While the words and activities of the craft degrees in the different rites vary, sometimes quite a bit, there is one common thread that runs through all the various rites and rituals — the legend of Hiram.

Now, before I write anything else, I have to throw in a disclaimer of sorts. Some time back I heard that a jurisdiction was thinking about removing the legend of Hiram from their ritual. As surprising as this information was, the reason behind their idea was even more remarkable. I was told that the reason for their wanting to remove this aspect of the ritual was because they could not establish if the legend of Hiram was a factual historical event. I was stunned. It's a *symbolic story* — a lesson. It is completely irrelevant if the story of Hiram is fact or fiction. Freemasonry is not teaching a history class. The story is used as a vehicle to deliver lessons of virtue and morality. The lessons that are taught are what is important, not the factual nature of the stories used to present the lessons. With that, we will continue.

The well-published story of Hiram takes place at the time of the building of King Solomon's Temple. We are taught that a great many Operative Masons worked on the construction of the

Temple. These Masons were guided in their work by three Grand Masters: King Solomon, King Hiram of Tyre, and the lead architect, Hiram Abif.

At some point, the three Grand Masters realized that a number of the craftsmen were performing their duties at such a high level of skill that it entitled them to special recognition. These craftsmen would be elevated to Master craftsmen. Now, in today's Freemasonry, if we receive a degree, an office or position of importance, we're honored by that advancement. But in reality, it means very little outside of our Masonic life. Our Freemasonry is *Speculative* Freemasonry, and it is something we do *outside* of our family life and chosen livelihood. This was not the same with the old Operative Freemasons. Freemasonry was their livelihood. It was how they fed their family and paid their bills. Being advanced to the rank of Master was a big deal. Not only did it mean an elevation in their social status, but it also meant a considerable pay increase. This advancement was a very important event in their life.

When the news of the pending advancements was made known, we can assume that considerable excitement and interest developed. It is because of the importance of these advancements to the lives of those receiving them that some concern among the Grand Masters developed. It seemed reasonable to put into place some sort of security measure so that individuals who did not deserve the advancement could not assume rank to which they were not entitled.

It was decided that a secret word would be given to all new Masters of the Craft so that they could prove their rank by possession of this word. As a further security measure, it was decided that this word would not be given out to anyone unless all three Grand Masters were present and agreed to the investiture.

The story goes on that three craftsmen obviously realized that they would likely *not* be elevated to a higher rank and were very unhappy about it. They wanted this advancement—badly. So much did they want this advancement that they hatched a plan to steal this "secret word," move to another area, and live their lives pretending to hold a rank that they did not earn.

They caught one of the Grand Masters alone and demanded that he tell them the secret word. Regardless of what they did, the Grand Master refused to give them this word. They became desperate. They made it clear to him that they were going to leave with either the word or him dead.

At this point, the Grand Master had a choice. He could give them what they wanted, or he could risk death. He took them seriously as his final words reflect acknowledgement of what he knew could happen.

And what happened next? Well, the ruffians made good on their threat, and they did kill him.

For a moment, stop and think about what happened. There is something that I was taught in childhood, and most likely, you have also been taught. It is that if I am ever in a situation where someone threatens my life in a robbery attempt, I should give them whatever they want. Why didn't he? I was taught that nothing I have on me is worth risking my life. Why didn't he just give them this word and then he could go on with his life?

The lesson of integrity is involved not because of a robbery attempt but because of an agreement that was made. This Grand Master agreed that he would not give the secret word to anyone unless certain conditions were met. Had these craftsmen attempted to simply rob him of some money, then it is reasonable that he would have freely exchanged whatever money he had on him for his life. But what these men wanted was something completely different. They demanded that he violate an agreement, his word.

Clearly the Grand Master recognized that he was not in control of their actions. He could not make them spare his life or do anything at all. Taking his life was something that they would either do or not do, and he had no control whatsoever over their actions. The only thing in which he had total control was *his* actions. They could take his life, but they could not take this word from him. He could only give it and that would be by *his* choice.

The Grand Master needed to determine what was of true value to him. He knew that we all live and die, but he also knew that *how* we live is up to us. To be robbed of some coins is no dishonor, but what of violating his word? What was that worth to him?

He did not agree to only give the word when certain conditions were met *unless* his life was threatened or only on the third Tuesday of the month if there was a full moon. He agreed to not give it unless these conditions were met. Period. If he gave the word to anyone and those conditions were not met, then he would be violating his word. It didn't matter if they offered him money, threatened him, or anything else. He would either keep his word or break it.

In life we can gain or lose material things. Because of the twists and turns in life we can amass great wealth or lose everything we own. Many things can happen to us because we were either in the right place or the wrong place. But either we have integrity and honor, or we do not. We have it because it is our choice, and we lose it also by choice.

Material things can be taken away from us, and we might have no choice in the matter — but not our integrity. We are the only ones who have the power to give our integrity away.

The Grand Master knew that we all live and die. He also knew that all of the magnificent structures that he helped create would mean nothing if his moral foundation was made of sand — void of integrity and honor. These men had the power to take his life, but they were powerless to make him live a life without integrity.

This was the point of the story — to teach a life lesson of virtue and morality, not to simply provide a historical account. But we should not believe that the story ends there.

The nature of symbolism is layered and often requires second and third looks to find deeper meanings. Just because we *believe* that we are acting with honor or integrity does not mean that this is actually the case. Let me give you an example.

A story from New Orleans in the early 1800s comes to mind. There were two men who were standing outside the St. Louis Cathedral having a friendly conversation. The two men were facing each other. One of the men felt a bit uncomfortable in his position and moved just a bit to the left to reposition himself.

When the man moved over, the other man winced in pain and looked shocked. In a sharp tone he demanded that the man return to his original position. The man who moved had no idea of what the other man was speaking, but he did not like his tone of voice.

What neither man realized nor considered was that the man who moved was considerably taller than the other man. In the position he was standing, he (unknown to either man) was standing right in a place where he was blocking the sun. When he moved a bit over, the sunlight hit the shorter man right in the eyes causing his painful reaction.

Neither man was of a mind to explain himself or ask too many questions of the other. Hot tempers took over and the friendly conversation was replaced by a very heated, nonsensical argument. And then it happened ... one man exclaimed that his "honor" had become compromised, and "integrity" demanded satisfaction.

He challenged the other man to a duel.

It was fortunate that neither man died in the duel, but one of them was shot in the arm. For the rest of his life, he lived with a useless arm as the result of the injury suffered in that duel. And for what? Honor? Integrity? One man moved a bit, and the other man had sun in his eyes. For that you shoot at each other?

What these men mistook for honor and integrity was pride, arrogance, and vanity. These vices were disguised as, or mistaken for, virtues.

There was no loss of honor in what happened, and integrity demanded nothing in the way of a duel. We must live our lives with honor and integrity. But we must know what a virtue is and what is a vice disguised as virtue. It's not always as clear as we think.

There will be times when we find it most difficult to understand or live up to our teachings. But, as we are so often told, it is the journey that is most important, not the final goal.

MASONIC COMMUNICATIONS

When I say something, the last thing I want is to be misunderstood. My goal is to always have the idea, thought, or desire in my head given to the other clearly and correctly. If I wanted someone to walk three houses down from where I live to a certain address and ask Mr. Jones if I can borrow a saw, it would not serve me very well if I pointed vaguely and said, "Go down there and bring me something from that guy." Where, what, who? If I want a particular thing (and not just anything), I need to be clear in communicating.

On the other hand, if I wish to teach using symbolism, then I will speak or write in a manner that will require the reader or listener to apply some thought to what I have offered. What is presented through symbolism may have more than one meaning and may not be evident by design. How I communicate depends on my desired goal. Language is a tool that should be employed with some thought as to the desired effect in each particular instance.

So, what exactly do we mean when we refer to "Masonic Communications"? This is a fundamental question, as we, as Freemasons, cannot engage in "Masonic Communications" with just anyone. We have certain obligations that we must uphold. It is crucial that we understand what can be communicated to others and what is not permissible.

Of "communication," Albert Mackey tells us:

> "The meeting of a Lodge is so called. There is a peculiar significance in this term. To communicate, originally meaning to share in common with others, was a common practice in Old English. The great sacrament of the Christian Church, which denotes a participation in the mysteries of the religion and a fellowship in the church, is called a communion, which is fundamentally the same as a communication, for he who partakes of the communion is said to communicate. Hence the meetings of Masonic Lodges are called communications, to signify that it is not simply the ordinary meeting of a society for the transaction of business, but that such meeting is the fellowship of men engaged in a common pursuit, and governed by a common principle, and that there is therein a communication or participation of those feelings and sentiments that constitute a true brotherhood."[1]

Our Work teaches us that we are not to hold "Masonic Communications" with non-Masons, or with unrecognized, irregular, or clandestine Masons. But what exactly does that mean to us today? It is clear through our law that someone who is a member of a lodge *not* in Fraternal Relations with our Grand Lodge cannot attend our meetings,[2] but what are we allowed to say (communicate) to non-Masons, and what is to be kept secret?

The Handbook of Masonic Law (Louisiana) tells us the following about the nature of a "secret":

> "Secrecy applies to the modes of recognition, certain symbols, the ballot, obligations, signs, passwords, and the forms of initiation."[3]

There we have it. We are not to reveal any of the above to anyone unless we are certain they are entitled to receive it. But who is entitled to receive it? We know that someone is entitled to receive "the secrets" if we have sat in lodge with them or if they have successfully passed a trial as taught to us in our ritual. Most jurisdictions will have similar rules, but to be safe, check with your Grand Lodge.

So, exactly who might be considered *unrecognized, irregular, or clandestine*? These are often words that are used in Masonry interchangeably — even officially by Grand Lodges. Are they really interchangeable? What exactly do they mean? While these words can mean the same thing, they each have their own specific meaning and can sometimes mean very different things. We can run into confusion if we do not know when they can or can't be used interchangeably.

Fraternal Relations (recognition) is when two jurisdictions officially declare their satisfaction that each is regular. It is a treaty of friendship and acknowledgment that each is a legitimate Masonic body. It is a state that either exists or does not. It is simple to determine. The Grand Lodge has a list of Masonic bodies which it "recognizes" and members who are allowed to visit our lodges, and with whom we may hold Masonic Communications — once we know them to be such. If a lodge is not on that list, it cannot visit tiled lodges under the jurisdiction of the Grand Lodge of Louisiana. But can we visit lodges with unrecognized Masons? Is there any situation where we can legally hold *Masonic Communications* with members of unrecognized lodges? The simple answer to the above questions is a surprising "yes" (at least in Louisiana, check your laws). It is sometimes called the "When in Rome Rule."

From the *Louisiana Handbook on Masonic Law*:

"Louisiana Masons, when traveling to other Grand Jurisdictions which are recognized as "Regular" by the

Grand Lodge of the State of Louisiana, F.&A.M. and with which this Grand Lodge has established fraternal relations may, with the consent of the host Lodge or Grand Lodge, visit a tiled communication in any Lodge recognized as Regular by the Grand Lodge of Louisiana, F.&A.M. within that jurisdiction and, during the course thereof, exercise Masonic visitation with the Brethren who are recognized as Regular by that Grand Jurisdiction."[4]

This law was put in place because the "mainstream" Grand Lodges in the United States have entered into Fraternal Relations with the Prince Hall Affiliate Grand Lodge in their state, with the vast majority doing so. They consider Prince Hall Affiliate Masons perfectly regular. Louisiana is one of the states that has not yet entered into Fraternal Relations with the Prince Hall Grand Lodge in our state. As such, if the "When in Rome Rule" did not exist in our Grand Lodge law, visiting any of the lodges in those other Grand Lodges that recognize Prince Hall in their state could be a problem. We could be sitting in a lodge and holding Masonic Communications with Masons not recognized by our Grand Lodge. That would be grounds for Masonic charges of violating our obligations. How could our Grand Master or other Grand Lodge Officers visit other jurisdictions? So, does this mean we view Prince Hall as regular or not?

Regularity is a subjective state. It is not as clear to determine as we might think, and certainly not as easy to determine as recognition. Grand Lodges, after examination, determine if a body is, or is not, *regular*, and views on regularity can change.

In an attempt to make the whole situation a bit easier to understand, Grand Lodges, years ago, seemed to become fond of linking regularity with recognition. If a body was recognized, then it was viewed as regular. It was said to be irregular or clandestine if it was not recognized. Most of the time, this worked fine. But every now and then, we are bitten if we never allow for the exception. The "When in Rome Rule" illustrates that we can't always rely on recognition to establish regularity. Logic dictates that if the Grand Lodge of Louisiana considers Prince Hall Affiliate Masonry to be irregular, then our law presents a situation where we are allowed to hold Masonic Communications with those we believe to be irregular. Is that what we are saying? That would seem to be a violation of our Obligations.

Louisiana has an official written record of viewing at least one Grand Lodge regular with whom Fraternal Relations had not yet been established. If we look at the Grand Lodge of Louisiana Proceedings from 1955, we can find that Louisiana considered the National Grand Lodge in France to be regular. Yet, Fraternal Relations were not then offered or existing.[5] Yep, they were deemed *regular*, but they were not *recognized*. Lack of recognition *does not* always officially mean irregular.

To be irregular means that there is something wrong with the body. It could be a problem with the work, the lineage (how they were created), or any other matter that would present a problem to anyone seeking to determine whether they are a valid Masonic body. It could be a minor, fixable problem or a problem of such severity that the body would be deemed hopeless and unable to be saved.

And what of the word "clandestine"? Yes, it is often used with or in place of "irregular." But it has a much more specific meaning. When the Soviet Union broke apart, an interesting thing happened. All of a sudden, hands started popping up. The hands belonged to Masonic lodges that had existed in the Soviet Union but were underground and hidden away. Freemasonry was outlawed, and had these lodges been discovered, the members would have been in considerable trouble. But they kept Freemasonry alive by working in secret. These are actual *clandestine* lodges — hidden lodges. Yes, they were irregular in the most technical sense as they operated under no Grand Lodge authority. But as soon as they were discovered, the European Grand Lodges lined up to take them in. They realized that the "problem" was an easy fix, and these Masons were worthy of great respect, not condemnation.

At the writing of this paper, Fraternal Relations between the Most Worshipful Grand Lodge of the State of Louisiana, F&AM, and the Most Worshipful Prince Hall Grand Lodge of Louisiana, F&AM does not exist. The law of the Grand Lodge of Louisiana is clear that members of lodges under any Grand Lodge with whom Fraternal Relations do not exist cannot sit in one of our tiled lodges. Yet, the law is also clear that situations can arise where it is permitted for members of lodges under the Grand Lodge of Louisiana to sit in tiled lodges with Masons under the jurisdiction of a Prince Hall Grand Lodge. When we sit in a tiled lodge, "Masonic Communications" (however we define it) is taking place. At the opening of this paper, I pointed out the problems that can arise when we are not clear about our desires. It would seem that a contradiction exists in our laws and obligations. On the one hand, we are clearly told that we *cannot* hold Masonic Communications with an unrecognized Mason. Yet, in another aspect of our law, we are told that we *are* allowed to hold Masonic Communications with unrecognized Masons under certain situations. Neither directive references the other nor explains the apparent contradiction.

Freemasonry in the United States is in a time of remarkable evolution. Electronic communications, in general, have dramatically changed with the advent of cell phones, the internet, and a host of new electronic gadgets. With the recognition of Prince Hall Masonry by most of the Grand Lodges in the United States, our understanding of Masonic Communications has, by practicality, undergone a reevaluation and resulted in an evolution of the practice. It is not a perfect solution and is open to numerous charges of contradictory and illogical practices, but it is a work in progress. It is a step.

Should the Grand Lodge of Louisiana and the Prince Hall Grand Lodge of Louisiana clear up this apparent contradiction and officially enter into Fraternal Relations? This writer has his personal opinion, but it is a question for the two Grand Lodges. What is it that they both desire?

Fraternal Recognition is a two-way street. *Both* sides must desire it and work towards its end. So, what do we want? It is a question we must all answer sooner or later.

Notes

1. Albert G. Mackey, *An Encyclopedia of Freemasonry and its Kindred Sciences Vol. I* (New York: The Masonic History Company, 1925) 170.

2. "One who is a member of a Lodge under the jurisdiction of a Grand Lodge not in fraternal relations with the Grand Lodge of Louisiana, shall not be permitted to visit any of the Lodge of Louisiana." *The Handbook of Masonic Law* (Alexandria, LA: The Grand Lodge of the State of Louisiana, F&AM 2012) 110.

3. Ibid., iv b

4. Ibid 110.

5. "We do not question the regularity of the French National Grand Lodge — their recognition by 41 of the Grand Lodges of the United States attests to that. We are not ready, however, to suggest that the Grand Lodge of Louisiana sever the cordial relationship of long standing with the Grand Lodge of France." *Proceedings of The Grand Lodge of the State of Louisiana Free and Accepted Masons* (New Orleans: Searcy & Pfaff, LTD., Printers, 1955) 180.

PERSONALIZING MASONIC SYMBOLISM

O ne of the things that I've always enjoyed about Freemasonry is its use of symbolism in Masonic education. I
appreciate how we use more or less common items to
represent a complex thought or object lesson. I know, of course,
that the use of symbols is far older than Freemasonry. The use of
symbolism as an educational tool can be traced back to the earliest
days of man.

But what I like about how we use symbolism in today's
Freemasonry is that we can almost personalize it to fit our own
needs. Since a symbol is essentially a memory aid, we can take
significant past personal events and turn them into our own
unique symbols for various Masonic teachings.

Let me give you an example by retelling a disturbing event in
my life that I use when I want to think of various Masonic moral
lessons.

I joined Freemasonry when I was 21. When I was in my late
20s, I decided that I wanted to move to California. So, I did. I
moved to the small town of Clovis. It was a nice place to live, not
far from the incredible beauty of Yosemite, and also not far from
the California coast — places like Carmel and Monterey. There was

even a Masonic lodge in Clovis that I would visit on a semi-regular basis. It was a good time. But then something very unexpected happened.

One Saturday morning, I was sipping my morning coffee and flipping through the newspaper. I saw an ad for an electronics store in a shopping center near my home. I had been eyeing some stereo speakers, and now they were on sale at a great price. I decided to jump in the car and go buy them.

I had about $120 cash on me. I drove to the shopping center and pulled into the parking lot. It was about 10 or 10:30 in the morning. I parked the car and got out. As I was walking to the back of the car, I saw something. A kid was standing there behind the car. He looked about sixteen or seventeen. As I looked closer at him, I noticed that he had a gun in his hand. I was not happy about seeing this gun pointing at me, but I was having trouble processing what I was seeing. I froze where I stood.

After what seemed to be an eternity (but was probably no more than a couple of seconds), the kid said, "I'll take your money." Everything was brought quickly into reality. I'm not exactly sure what I was thinking, but I didn't have a lot of money, and I really wanted to buy those speakers. I didn't want to give him my money, so I told him I didn't have any on me. He cocked the gun.

The gun was a revolver, and I could see the cylinder turning as the weapon was being cocked. The barrel seemed to get larger as I looked at it. It started to look like he was pointing a cannon at me. I remember thinking to myself, "What's wrong with you? Don't play around with him. Just give him what he wants!"

I told him, "OK," then I reached into my pocket and handed him the money. He took it and just stared at me. I looked in his eyes, and they were just ... empty. There was no emotion, no expression — nothing. They were blank, dead eyes.

Then he said, "You shouldn't have lied to me." I remember a cold feeling coming over me, and I was thinking, "Oh God, this kid is going to shoot me." I felt helpless. He just stared at me with an odd half-grin.

All kinds of thoughts crossed my mind, and nothing added up. I had no idea how I ended up in this situation. Then, just when I expected to be shot, I saw his eyes dart to his left — right over my right shoulder. A look of shock came over his face. He spun around and was gone. He didn't say a word. He just took off running.

I was stunned, and my first thought was "Police!" I turned around, fully expecting to see a police car or cops running up on foot. But there was nothing. I looked all around. I saw no cars or people anywhere behind me. The closest building was a bank that was towards the end of the mostly empty parking lot, but no one was anywhere around.

I was completely confused and quite shaken. I have no idea why he took off running like he did. I have no idea if he saw someone who took off themselves or what happened. All I knew was that I was fortunate to be alive.

I went home, and "what if?" was all that I could think about. I did a lot of thinking about my life, where I was, where I wanted to go, and how quickly all that I had planned for the years ahead could have ended. Yeah, I did a lot of thinking.

It was clear that I was given a second chance. A few days later, I realized that the lodge in town was having a meeting. I decided to go visit them. I had missed the last few meetings and just wanted to be in a Masonic atmosphere.

Having no idea what was on the evening's schedule, I showed up. As it turns out, the lodge had scheduled a Master Mason degree. I was, needless to say, moved and affected by what I saw in the first and especially the second section.

While the lessons taught in the Master Mason degree focus, in part, on integrity or the test of integrity, my own situation involved no such "test." It was an armed robbery — nothing more. But it made me think a great deal about life itself.

Every single one of us will one day die. We have no choice in this matter. We also have no idea when that day will come. All over the world, many people were alive yesterday, planning for their future, and who are not with us today. We will never know what plans they may have had that were lost today.

While we have no power over death, there are things that we can do in life.

Until the time of our death, we have total control over our own actions. When that kid had his gun pointed at me, it seemed that he was in control of me. But really, he wasn't. I realized that the money in my pocket wasn't worth dying for, so I chose to give it to him. There was no loss of integrity in my action. I had not given my word that I would not give anyone the money unless certain conditions were met. But what if I had? Then it would have been a matter of integrity. I would have had to make a very quick decision about whether my life was worth my integrity.

That was the test in the Master Mason degree. Hiram realized that we all live and die. It was discovered that no one can take our integrity. We are the only ones who can give away our integrity or keep it. It is a powerful lesson. It calls for uncompromising self-examination and unyielding resolve.

But the lessons of that degree involve more than integrity. The overall lessons involve choices that we make and *when* we make them. We have the freedom to go down any life path that we choose. In fact, if we choose one path and decide later that it is not the right one for us, we can choose another direction. We can do this again and again all the way up until the moment of our death.

But when we die, we become locked in whatever path we were on. There is no going back to redo or improve things. The lesson here is to think and choose well. Some choices may be our last.

Another lesson would seem to be responsibilities — the ones we have to ourselves and others. Believe me, if you are under the impression that it is your duty in Freemasonry to gain or maintain power, glory, titles, and degrees (or to prop up those who do believe this), then you are most definitely on the wrong path. We are not about trying to impress others with any "VIP degree or office." The goal of Freemasonry is to take a good man and give him the tools by which he can improve himself. We are to learn and grow. We grow by improving our minds, skills, and morality.

But why do we do that?

I mean, it's a nice idea, but is that all there is to Freemasonry? I don't believe it is. We have a far deeper responsibility. Masonry is not all about us. We must learn how to help others. We are not in this world alone.

A good man, however, can't wave his hand and *make* others good. We can only change ourselves. We have no ability to make others do what we want them to do. We can only control *our* actions. What we can do is learn, live, and radiate the lessons of Freemasonry. We can't force anyone down any life path, but we can be an inspiration to others. We can be the person who inspires others to take a different, better path — if they choose to do so. We can do that.

We have a responsibility to ourselves and the world to help others as we can. Unfortunately, there is a catch. We can make all the most wonderful plans in the world for next year, next month, or even tomorrow. But if tonight is our last night on this Earth, then all our good plans are wasted. The lesson is that if we want to do something, we need to do it *now* because tomorrow may never come.

In music, we may know all the proper notes to play. But if our timing is off, then the music will not sound as it should. Timing truly is everything. In all of life, timing is everything. It's not enough to know the right thing to do. We must do it, and we have to do it at the right time.

If we don't care, then nothing matters. But if we do care, then we must accept the reality, responsibility, and the choices in life.

Planning to do the right thing tomorrow may result in being forever known as the guy who refused to do the right thing. All action should be taken now. But, as in all things, the choice is ours.

THE RITUAL

I have long believed that within our ritual is the core of our Masonic teachings. The rituals are much more than a play designed to entertain the membership. In fact, when the ritual is degraded to the point it is viewed as entertainment by the membership, our Masonic initiation is also degraded to the point that it becomes meaningless. There are few things more shameful than members of a lodge entertaining themselves at the expense of a candidate. Not only is the opportunity for meaningful initiation lost to the candidate, but the lodge is reduced to a nonsensical merriment club. Our candidates, the lodge, and our rituals deserved more.

Since learning aspects of the ritual in our catechism is required by all who join,[1] all Masons have some familiarity with our ritual. Of course, knowing the catechism necessary to advance through the degrees does not make one a ritualist. But learning the ritual does give the opportunity to spot a ritualist. Those with a knack for ritual can be easily identified by how they handle the memorization of the catechism. But what exactly is the role of a ritualist in the lodge?

A ritualist in the lodge is one who has proven that he knows the ritual work and the lodge has confidence in him to perform and teach the ritual. During a degree, a ritualist will be one who takes a "speaking part" in the degree, if needed, or acts as a "supervisor" (prompter) if any of the officers forget lines. A ritualist will also serve as a lodge instructor for new members going through the degrees.

The lodge's view of our Masonic ritual falls into three main categories. This would be how the lodge members view the importance and meaning of the ritual. One group is those who do not care about good ritual or what the ritual means; another group is those who care about good ritual but believe that the meaning of the ritual is not very important; and the final group is those who do care about good ritual and what the ritual means or teaches us.

When we visit a lodge, its nature or personality can often be determined rather quickly. Most successful lodges will have members who, before the lodge meeting, will seem in good humor, and enjoyable conversations will be taking place between the brothers, maybe over a meal. This atmosphere of enjoyment is necessary for any lodge wishing to survive, but it itself is not a guarantee of success. It doesn't matter if the lodge is formal in nature, sometimes called Traditional Observance, or if the lodge is casual and truly little more than a social club. A successful lodge can be defined by its membership and their desires. But once the time comes for the lodge meeting to start, we have the opportunity to see the true nature of the lodge.

The first thing that is noticed is how the officers are dressed and act in their stations. They may be dressed up, maybe not in tuxes, but in a coat and tie or, at the very least, nice slacks and shirts. These officers will assume their stations with an air of responsibility and confidence. When the meeting starts, they will deliver their parts of the ritual for the opening letter-perfect or near letter-perfect. They will act dignified in these stations, with all present fully aware that what is taking place is significant and meaningful. This will be a lodge that is taken seriously. Of course, this type of lodge is not the only type of lodge that can be successful. We do find lodges where the officers come to their stations in jeans or other casual attire. They often joke and laugh just prior to the opening and assume the stations casually. The opening ritual is often marred by errors, necessitating prompting for most officers. Learning the ritual is not a priority for them, nor is it the primary reason for their involvement in the lodge.

Mind you, we are only talking about successful lodges. A failing lodge may operate exactly the same, but that is a different story. There are successful casual lodges that operate more like social clubs, with minimal expectations or desires from or *for* the members.

In my experience, a common thread in all casual or social club lodges is the apparent disregard that they have for learning the ritual. The ritual is just something that needs to be muddled through to open the meeting. It plays no other role in the lodge function and could easily be done away with in this type of lodge setting.

On the other end of the spectrum is the lodge where the ritual is viewed as the cornerstone of the lodge. The ritual is not only learned by the officers, but its meaning is taught to all the membership in classes during lodge meetings. It is realized, in these lodges, that within the ritual are symbolic teachings of the lodge, and these teachings are expounded to the membership.

The primary difference between these two types of lodges lies in their purposes: one serves as a social club, while the other is dedicated to teaching the lessons of Freemasonry. Both types of lodges can be successful depending on what the members want. Each type of lodge must understand itself, the type of lodge that it has, and recognize that this is what they want out of their Masonic experience.

What I have found is that problems can come with the third type of lodge. This lodge professes the ritual's importance but fails to teach its meaning or require officers to be proficient in it. This type of lodge does not honestly acknowledge its own nature nor understand or accept what is necessary to be something else.

As with everything in life, we have choices in Freemasonry. We can choose whatever path we want. We can participate in whatever type of Masonry we want. We can also lie to ourselves. We can go down a path that is clearly painted green and tell the whole world, and ourselves as well, that it is painted blue. We have that right and that ability.

There is nothing wrong with belonging to a lodge that is little more than a social club. Many social club lodges do wonderful charitable work. They are made up of members who would, if needed, give you the shirt off their back. They are good men. However, they do not take advantage of the deeper lessons in Freemasonry. These lodges do not study the ritual or use it as part of their regular education program of self-improvement. They simply go to the lodge, enjoy a meal, talk with their friends, read bills during the meeting, and discuss plans for various programs. There is nothing wrong with that, but the simple truth is that this was not the original plan or goal of Freemasonry. It is a stripped-down modification of the original design. Those who recognize and accept this can establish a successful lodge of this nature. They have selected a path to travel and are satisfied with it.

The lodges that teach Masonic education do the work that Freemasonry was designed to do, and have also selected a path. They understand what they want to do, what they need to do to achieve it, and do the work necessary to achieve their goals of self-improvement.

Both of these types of lodges have picked a lane; they have selected a path to travel. They both can be successful as long as they understand what they are and what they are not. They can work well as long as they stay in their lane and continue on their chosen path.

It is that third group of lodges that has the most trouble. These are the ones who do not understand what or who they are. They are unclear about what is necessary for them to do, and they also fail to properly understand the direction they wish to take.

They often fall into a ritual trap that leads to internal frustration and an inability to achieve their goals, despite their apparent hard work.

The third type of lodge falls into the trap of believing all is well when all is far from well. The problem comes from a false belief about the ritual as well as the role that members play in the leadership of the lodge. In the *Old Charges of a Mason*, there is an interesting line: "no Master or Warden is chosen by seniority, but for his merit." What does *merit* mean? What is considered merit if not seniority? Does it mean leadership abilities? Sure, sounds like it does. So then, should we consider someone good in business to be excellent material for a lodge officer? Maybe, maybe not.

In Operative Masonry, the leaders were chosen by those who were considered the most skilled craftsmen. Those who were best able to do the work were also best capable of leading others in the work. But what is "the work" of Speculative Masonry? This is where it becomes necessary to pick a lane and decide on the path for a lodge. If "the work" is the education of our candidates and members, then we take one path. If "the work" is limited to enjoying lodge activities and possibly some charitable work, then we take a different approach. Both paths have successful lodges.

The problem comes when we try to have the best of both worlds. If we desire to be a lodge where real Masonic education takes place, but we operate as a social club, then we are doomed before we start. This situation brings constant frustration for all involved. In my experience, I've seen too many lodges that simply cannot pick a lane and seem to want to be one thing, but are not willing to do what is needed to be what they want.

I'll give a few observations that I have gleaned over the years. First, not everyone has to be a lodge officer. The idea that one is not really worthy unless they have a "PM" behind their name is nonsense. We are not about gaining titles and honors. We are about learning and teaching. Second, not every good businessman is a good lodge officer. Running a multi-million dollar business does not guarantee that you will be a good lodge leader any more than being a good lodge leader will qualify you to run a large, successful business. It's apples and oranges. In my opinion, the belief that business experience qualifies one for lodge leadership is a primary reason lodges often go off in the wrong direction. So, what makes a good lodge leader?

It goes back to the blueprint laid out in the *Old Charges*. The best leaders have the best abilities. They are the ones who are best able to do the work. The work is, in the broad sense, the ritual, but we must be careful of the trap. If we view "the ritual" as the few lines of opening and closing the lodge, then we are trapped. Knowing the ritual encompasses not only the opening and closing, but also all the degrees of the ritual, as well as its underlying meanings. The officers must be able to teach the meaning of the ritual to the young candidates. I mean, *any* of the officers must be able to do this. They must all be able to stand in for any other officer and teach any of the rituals.

Many lodges feel, and rightly know, that such an expectation is too much for their lodge. Not everyone can learn the ritual, but all lodges need officers every year. It is simply too much to expect all the officers to know all the rituals in a manner that they are not only considered proficient (or near it), but also can teach their meaning. They just can't do it.

So, what happens? What do such lodges do? Well, let's try to find that answer by looking at something else. What if you genuinely, deeply, and passionately want to be a concert pianist? You went to piano class occasionally, but had other interests. You never learned to play very well at all. But you still want to be a concert pianist. Guess what? That's not going to happen. So, you can be frustrated all your life, or you can join a music club and try to enjoy some of the music's benefits. At some point, we have to get real.

Not every lodge can, wants to, or needs to be an educational, formal Masonic lodge. A successful lodge can be one where its members simply enjoy each other's company. Everyone needs to be dead honest with themselves and properly evaluate themselves so that they can get the most out of every Masonic experience. We need to know ourselves, understand who we are and what we are, and always strive to be better tomorrow than we are today — by whatever standard we use.

Notes

1. At least, in U.S. jurisdictions of which I am familiar.

Masonic Memory Work

Recently, I was contacted by a young man who told me that he was in a difficult situation. He said that he had petitioned a lodge and just received notice that he was balloted on and passed the ballot. He said that he was told that he would soon receive his initiation. But what would follow the initiation is what concerned him.

The young man said that when the investigation committee visited him, they told him that following each degree, he would need to memorize a catechism and then stand an examination in open lodge. He would need to recite what he memorized. That worried him. He expressed extreme concern about this, as he disliked speaking in public and struggled with memory work. He was afraid that he would fail horribly.

I told the young man that the purpose of the memory work in Freemasonry is not to embarrass him or to ensure we have copies of our ritual. We have printed rituals safely stored away. The purpose of doing memory work is to emphasize that we value things we've earned more than those given as gifts or prizes. It's a way for us to internalize and understand the teachings of our fraternity, and it's a tradition that has been passed down for generations.

In Freemasonry, we should work for what we receive. The memory work expected of new Masons is not designed to put anyone on the spot, nor is the work expected to be letter-perfect. What is expected is that the candidate demonstrates a strong work ethic in fulfilling the requirements.

Regarding his concerns about being up to the job of memory work, I advised him to give it his best shot. Everyone there wants only to help him. The members of the lodge are not there to torment or criticize, but to support and guide. I told him that a side benefit of this type of work is that it serves as mental exercise, which in itself helps everyone.

I told him that the mind is a powerful tool and can do more for us than we might imagine. The mind can open doors for us by expanding our capabilities, but it can also limit us if we don't use it wisely. A strong mind is our friend. A weak mind is not.

In discussing memory work and the mind, a story I read years ago about memory may be of some value.

One summer, a young boy was visiting India with his family. One of the things the boy looked forward to doing was riding an elephant. So, they went to a place that offered elephant rides.

When he first saw the elephants, he was absolutely awestruck at how huge they were. As he was looking around, however, he noticed that no fences were keeping them from roaming off. He saw that they were all tied with a rope around their ankles, and the rope was staked to the ground. But even as a boy, he knew that something was wrong with the rope that was being used. It looked thin and weak for these massive elephants. He didn't understand why they couldn't easily snap the ropes and just walk off.

The boy asked a worker about the ropes. The worker told him that the elephants had been with them since they were first born. As very young elephants, these ropes were strong enough to hold the small animals. They didn't have the strength or size to break the ropes ... at that time.

Now, elephants have good memories, but they don't always seem to use them to their best advantage. You see, as adults, they are large enough and strong enough to break the ropes, but they remember being young and how the ropes held them fast. They remember the past and *believe* that the ropes will not break. They think that these are very strong ropes, so they don't even bother trying to break free.

The elephants have very good memories, but they don't always apply logic to their memories. They use their memory but not their minds. In Freemasonry, we are encouraged to use both our memory and our mind. The story of the elephants serves as an important lesson for all of us, reminding us that we should not be limited by our past experiences, but use our minds to overcome challenges and grow.

In Masonry, the use of the mind is essential to all facets of our teachings. Yes, we are taught the importance of memory, but also of using the mind to our best advantage. We can apply reason, intelligence, and logic to memory. We can believe that we can or can't do things. Of course, we can believe all day long that we can flap our arms and fly ... but we can't. But there are so many things that we *can* do if we only believe and apply ourselves.

The Masonic memory work expected of candidates is not busy or nonsense work. It is a valuable and integral part of our teachings, designed to lay a solid foundation for future lessons. These are lessons that we can either take advantage of and grow from, or we can do only the basics and belong to a club.

So, for the young men about to join and worrying about doing the memory work, relax. The members of the lodge are not here to play games with you. They are on your side, ready to support and guide you. These are your friends and soon to be your brothers.

Freemasonry is not some 2nd rate college fraternity looking to have fun. We are a system of morality, veiled in allegory, and illustrated by symbols. These words do mean something. Soon, you will get to see how and why, and it will inspire and enlighten you.

CHARITY?

A Mason spoke with me about something I had written a while back. I had mentioned that Freemasonry is not a club. It's not a social, civil, or charitable club. He said that if charity has no role in Freemasonry, then why does it seem important in our ritual? I pointed out that there is a difference between acting as a charitable person and being a charitable club or organization. It also dawned on me that the whole concept of charity might need to be revisited.

To start with, Freemasonry is both a philosophy and an organization. Our philosophy involves symbolic lessons designed to help individuals who are fundamentally good make improvements in their lives. The philosophy of Freemasonry exists apart from the organization of Freemasonry, but it is a vital part of the organization. Without the philosophy of Freemasonry, the organization does, indeed, become a club.

Charity is one of the philosophical lessons of Masonry. But Freemasonry itself is not a charitable organization or club. We have a different role. Professional charitable organizations such as the United Way, Red Cross, Salvation Army, Habitat for Humanity, and many others exist to raise and distribute money and aid to those in need. That is their reason for existing. Freemasonry does not exist for the sole purpose of extending charity.

Having said the above, Freemasonry, or should I say, *Freema-sons*, are known for extending charity when needed. But, just as there is some confusion as to whether Freemasonry is a charitable organization, there is a misunderstanding about charity itself. I'd like to take a closer look at the act of charity. There are times when charity might be of far less actual help than we might believe. It is this misunderstanding that may contribute to how some people (as well as some Masons) become confused as to Freemasonry's role in charity.

Those who need charity seem to fall into two categories — those who have just come into need and those who have been in need for some time. Right after a flood, hurricane, tornado, or some other disaster, there will be people in need of help. They were going along with their lives, and out of the blue, something unexpected happened, and everything was lost. They need help now. Charity towards them usually comes in the manner of food, temporary housing (if needed), and medical needs. Normally, this type of need arises so quickly that most who extend charity do so without really thinking about it. This is also where any of the many professional charitable organizations shine. Meal wagons arrive, offering hot food. Shelters open where the needy can sleep, have a shower, and access other essential services. Community aid normally soon pops up. People in the area unaffected by the disaster donate extra clothing and food from their pantries. The immediate needs of the suffering are relieved, and they can then go about rebuilding their lives. But it is different for those who have been suffering for some time. The reality of long-term poverty and need can sometimes require a different kind of char-ity. Sometimes the "charity" we give is more about our own feelings of satisfaction than about providing real help to those in need. Let me give you an example.

I watched a video about a celebrity who was being praised for his act of charity in giving food and aid to a small village in Africa. Apparently, he had seen the suffering taking place in numerous villages on TV. According to the report, he showed up in this village without notice, bearing gifts. He flew into the village with a large supply of fast-food hamburgers in heated containers, bottles of water, and t-shirts. He tossed the t-shirts out to the crowd of happy, waving villagers. He then passed out the hamburgers and water. Make no mistake, they truly were delighted and appreciative of the gifts. The cameras showed the many smiling faces and the overall poverty of the village. The people felt good. The celebrity felt good, and the event was praised by all. But what was the real goal? Was the goal to truly help these people? If so, he may not have done as well as he may have believed or could have done.

Now, I don't want to seem to be throwing cold water on anyone, but I'd like to take a real, honest look at the needs and charity extended. Maybe something might have been missing. I'd like to reexamine the two examples of charity given above.

With any type of disaster, people are suddenly thrown into a state of immediate need. Maybe they required no aid the day before, but once the disaster happened, they were in real, serious trouble. Their everyday lives were thrown upside down. Without assistance, they may die because of the disaster. The gifts of food, clothing, and shelter were what were needed to help them. This type of charity holds people in this condition up while they can get their lives in order and rebuild. Because of the aid, they can return to their former lives, or close to it.

A poverty-stricken village is a different matter. Their crisis is having nothing at all. But the difference is that it did not happen all of a sudden. Their condition had existed for a long time. It is the reality of how they live. Bringing food and gifts to them did help them at the moment. But the very next day, they will be hungry again. They would still be poor and in need. I'm sure that the celebrity had all good intentions. He saw images of very hungry people. He must have thought he had enough money to go there and bring them some food. He acted out of kindness. However, as he was not a professional in a charitable organization, he was unsure how to provide the most effective help in this situation.

The celebrity bought burgers for the village. He fed them for one day. Had he gone to the village ahead of time and spoken to the people there, maybe he could have taken that same money and bought some new tools and seed for the farmers. That would help feed the villagers for maybe several seasons. Perhaps instead of investing in t-shirts, he could have given the money needed for a few medical supplies or equipment. Maybe he could have invested in something that could help their economy. The celebrity had a good heart, but his lack of involvement in charity work meant he did not fully grasp the real needs.

Freemasonry is not a charitable organization. We are not trained in this type of aid, and when we involve ourselves in any kind of long-term aid to any in need, we can run into trouble. Yes, Freemasons can provide much-needed help in times of disaster. I have seen photos of whole lodges going out to a stricken community, helping with clean up or rebuilding after a disaster. But they are usually operating as individual Freemasons and under the direction of actual professionals working for charitable organizations.

We must understand that professional charitable organizations train their workers in the ways to provide the best assistance to individuals in need, depending on the situation. They know what to do and are not sidetracked by the emotion of the situation. Freemasonry provides none of this training. We don't provide this training because we are not a charitable organization. When we attempt to take on the role of a charitable organization without the necessary training, we can end up doing more harm than good. And that's even with the harm being done with all good intentions.

I saw a video clip of a TV actor who got himself in some trouble. He played a doctor on TV, went on a talk show, and gave medical advice. He's an actor, not a doctor. Putting all legal issues aside, he could have harmed someone by offering advice that, although appealing to him, was medically incorrect. Freemasons are taught to help others on a personal basis and in times of need. If we lack training, we can't assume the knowledge needed to plan for meaningful aid to those in long-term serious need. We can, of course, donate to organizations that do this type of work. We can volunteer to feed the needy in a soup kitchen. We can do all kinds of things to help others. We can and should do these things. We simply cannot act as if we are something we are not.

"Know thyself."

Inscribed on the frontispiece of the Temple of Delphi.

TRUST

Someone once told me that people born in a city are far more suspicious than country folk. I grew up in a city, but on a military base (my father was an Army Colonel), so I was never really sure as to how my thinking was defined. But I do know that when I joined Freemasonry, my thinking on pretty much everything changed. Right out of the gate, I was put in the care of someone who I had no choice but to trust. I knew full well that, if he wanted to, he could make a tremendous fool out of me. But he didn't. I could tell by the tone of his voice and his actions that he was worthy of trust.

Following my initiation, I was told that everything that happened was designed to teach (among other things) a lesson of trust. I was told that we can, and should, trust our brothers because they are our brothers. That brought back a flood of memories of my grandfather, who died when I was only 12. He was the reason that I wanted to become a Mason. One of the things that I remember about him was something that he said about Freemasonry and trust. He said that he would trust a Mason he did not know alone in his home with all his valuables. Was he foolish, or did he know something that many miss?

My father was a WWII veteran. I remember him talking about trust and those with whom he served in combat. He said that trust in those around you during that time was absolutely necessary. He said that to survive, you had to be completely sure the guy next to you had your back and would be there when needed. He said that when the fighting started, their training kicked in, and everything that they did was a result of their training. He trusted them because he knew how they were trained and that they were worthy of trust. I thought a lot about what he said.

A friend of mine served in Vietnam. He told a different story. He said that towards the end of the conflict, when new troops came in, they were immediately sent to the front. None of the ones who had been around a while wanted to be anywhere near them. When I asked him why, he said that it was because they were dangerous. Towards the end of the conflict, basic training was minimal. The ones who had been around a while knew that the training of the new guys was so lacking that not only would they likely get themselves killed, but all those around them. I found that as interesting as what my father had told me.

I've been a Mason now for fifty years. Just like I have changed in that time, so has Freemasonry changed. Some changes are for the good and some not so good. One of the "not so good" changes was our fear of declining membership some years back. Lodges were losing members and failing to attract new ones to replace them. We started taking in some who we may have rejected not long ago. We also began moving those who joined into leadership positions before they even knew the difference between a Landmark and a pancake breakfast. We traded education for fellowship. While we may not have seen it, we slowly started becoming something else—something very different than Freemasonry. To make it worse, the change came on so slowly that most of us didn't even notice it.

Make no mistake, Freemasonry has serious problems. The lack of training for too many of our members has resulted in them viewing Freemasonry as merely a social group. Too many do not understand who or what we are, and this lack of understanding allows fellowship combined with bad judgment to create seriously damaging situations. Our choice is to deal with the problems or watch our foundation crumble.

Recently, I read of a young girl who was attacked by an alligator. While being bitten, this child had the presence of mind to shove both of her thumbs into the alligator's nostrils. She remembered that this was what she was told to do if she was ever attacked. The alligator, unable to breathe, opened its mouth, allowing her to free herself and escape. We need the same calm, presence of mind. We need the balance of both competent Masonic education and the backbone to reduce the unruly to order, to do what is needed. Weakness in either area can result in our failure.

As for trust, there may be another straightforward reason as to why we have any trust at all in others. We trust because it feels good. Some scientists say that when we trust someone, our brains release Oxytocin. Oxytocin is a hormone that promotes pleasurable feelings. We want to feel good, and we want to be around those who make us feel good. In other words, we have a fundamental need to trust others because it's good for us. But on the flip side, we also have something of a sixth sense concerning dishonesty that may be able to protect us from trusting the wrong people. Concordia University in Montreal published a study by researchers in their psychology department, which found that children as young as fourteen months can differentiate between a credible person and a disingenuous one.[1] It's called balance. We want to trust others, but we seem to have an innate ability to know when trust is not deserved.

My father trusted those around him in WWII because he knew they had received proper training. My friend lost trust in those around him during the latter part of the Vietnam War because he questioned their training. Far too often, even the Masters of lodges are entirely unable to answer the most basic questions on the history, philosophy, laws, or customs of Freemasonry. It is very reasonable to question their "training." Is it any wonder that trust is lacking in Masonry? If we fail or are unable to trust our brothers, then we tear at the fabric of who we claim to be. We want to trust our brothers, we need to trust our brothers, and if we can't, it damages us at our core.

As with most things, Freemasons have a choice. We can act, or we can sit back and do nothing. I believe that inaction seals a very bad fate for us. But I also believe that to do the wrong thing will bring equally undesirable results. I believe that the ability to know right from wrong comes from our training — our teachings. It's not enough that we say that we are Freemasons; we need to be Freemasons. We need to know who and what we are and show it. We are seriously sick, and we need to take some possibly bad-tasting medicine. We need proper Masonic education. We need to make sure that all our members (especially those who lead us) understand our unique laws, customs, words, phrases, and philosophy. We need to be firm about this education. Without education or "training," we cannot trust our brothers. As difficult as it may seem, those who cannot or do not wish to learn cannot lead us in any manner. We simply cannot trust an untrained Mason. The choice as to what we do about our current situation is ours. I hope that we are wise.

Notes

1. https://www.researchgate.net/publication/266137801_You_Seem_Certain_but_You_Were_Wrong_Before_Developmental_Change_in_Preschoolers'_Relative_Trust_in_Accurate_versus_Confident_S-peakers

Why Didn't Hiram Fight Back?

I've written more than a few papers on the legend of Hiram. The reason for returning to this subject so often is that this legend presents the Masonic instruction of integrity so brilliantly. Like all great symbolic lessons, the Hiramic Legend can also be viewed from different angles. In one viewing, we see one example, and in another, we see something very different but equally important.

Not long ago, I received an interesting question. I was asked if I believed that Hiram needed to die to teach anything about integrity. The brother questioned if the lesson of integrity would have been compromised if Hiram had refused to give them what they wanted, but still fought back to save his life. Well, no, I don't believe that the moral would be compromised, but let's look at this question.

To start with, it should again be pointed out that this is a work of fiction. There is no evidence that this story of Hiram is an actual historical account. Masonry offers it as a vehicle to teach symbolic moral lessons. But any symbolic lesson worth anything has layers of lessons that can be drawn from it — even ones that were not originally written into it.

So, if we take the legend at face value, then Hiram was the Grand Master of a group of Operative Freemasons. We can take this to mean that he was a highly skilled Operative Freemason. He would have worked his way up from an apprentice. Then, based on his overall skill, he would have been selected as the leader of all the Masters — the Grand Master.

Hiram's work and path would have been long and hard. He would likely have been middle-aged or a bit past middle-aged to advance to the point he reached. He likely spent most of his life doing strenuous physical labor from sunrise to sunset.

As to the three "bad guys," well, they were not yet Masters. They were young and undoubtedly in good physical shape from years of hard work. They were not inexperienced apprentices.

While there is no suggestion that Hiram was feeble, he was certainly not in the same physical shape he was in during his youth. To take on three young men in their prime might have been a lot to expect from him. But, on the other hand, while Hiram was older and no longer in the same physical shape that he once was, why, indeed, would he not at least put up some fight against individuals who threatened to kill him? This is where symbolic moral lessons come into play.

A quality leader is always looking for those who can replace him. The only way that any organization or group can maintain its existence over the years is to have a constant stream of quality leaders with the organization's best interests at heart. Those leaders who prioritize their own interests above all else are the cancer within any group. The power-hungry, ego-driven leader is the weak link in any chain, regardless of any bravado they might display. So, how does a quality leader look for his replacements?

Elite military or law enforcement leaders often come up through the ranks and undergo extensive training. I recently watched something on military training that caught my attention. It was a Navy SEAL talking about leaders and an event during a training operation when he was one of the new guys. It was training that they had participated in many times before. They were to clear a building.

Everyone in this training exercise was focused on their current task and the next steps they would take. A threat could pop up anywhere and anytime. They entered a room, all looking down the barrels of their weapons, waiting for the instructor's next call. They waited. And they waited longer. But no instructions came.

The group of trainees began to realize that they were waiting too long, doing nothing. In an actual combat situation, this could be a problem. Finally, this new guy couldn't stand it any longer. He knew something was wrong. He then did something on his own.

The new guy pointed his weapon at the ceiling and took a step back. Then he looked around. He could see his platoon commander, the assistant commander, and everyone else, all frozen, looking down the barrels of their weapons. He then looked around at the whole area. He could see what needed to be done after taking a step back and looking at the entire situation. But no one gave the call.

Calling up his courage, he yelled out: "Hold Left! Clear Right!"

It was a basic command they had done many times before, and one he knew was correct for this situation. He expected someone to yell back, "Shut up! Who are you?!" Instead, he heard the command repeated, and they began executing just like they had done so many times. When it was over, he said that he fully expected one of the senior guys to chew him out for stepping out of line, but they just came up and told him, "Good job stepping up."

You see, it was a test. The point was that a leader or leaders giving the commands could be taken out at any moment. What happens to the team after that? If no one steps up, then they all may be lost. This test was to find potential future leaders. They needed to see who would first step up and then, second, give the correct call.

There is a lesson here for us all.

We don't need leaders in Freemasonry who don't know what they are doing. All the ego and loud talk in the world does not replace knowledge of Freemasonry. We also don't need leaders who fear stepping up, even when things are difficult. A leader must have the courage to do the right thing, even when he may be risking it all.

From just these points, Hiram would have displayed all the qualities of a true quality leader. According to what we know, Hiram displayed tremendous courage when facing those who would end up murdering him. He didn't give them what they wanted. He didn't violate his promises.

But the story does not tell us if he put up any fight to save his life. That may not be necessary to the story, but it is an interesting question. Let's try to find out if there could be more to this story.

Hiram may not have had great personal knowledge of the three bad guys, but we can assume that he at least knew them. He knew that they were not among the ones slated for advancement. If we delve into the realm of all things possible, then upon first seeing them, Hiram may have desired to test them further.

There is no clear answer with Hiram because the situation is not addressed in the story. All we can do is try to build on what we know and don't know. The test for the Navy SEALS was for the leader to do nothing at all so that he may see who steps up and does the right thing.

Hiram was a quality leader. He would have always been looking for those who could fill the leadership shoes in the future. While it's not explained why Hiram acted and did not act in certain ways during this confrontation, it is a fascinating study of human nature. I don't have any obvious or provable answers to the question, but it is not impossible that Hiram's last moments alive were spent thinking of the welfare of the Order from more than one position.

Hiram may have hoped that the bad guys could be redeemed at the last moment. It didn't happen, but it would show a unique quality in Hiram that he never gave up hope in his workers, even when hope was a very long shot. It would display a unique kindness and unyielding loyalty to the members.

From this story's outcome, we know that not all who are tested are worthy. Unworthy craftsmen need to be identified and kept from our inner circles. When given every chance, some will consistently choose the wrong path. They will put themselves and their own best interest first. But Hiram chose the right path from every way you view this situation.

The story is worth looking at and thinking about over and over. These moral lessons contain hidden gems that we may only find with a close examination. As with so very many of the Masonic symbolic lessons, you only need to study them a bit.

THE BALLOT BOX

Recently, I've had conversations with several Masons concerning problems we have today in Freemasonry. One Mason mentioned that we need to face the fact that many of today's problems began a good number of years ago, with declining membership. He said that, due to concerns about dwindling numbers, we did not pay close enough attention to who joined us. He said that because we did not properly guard the West Gate, too many joined who should not have been allowed to enter. They have now worked their way into all positions in all Masonic bodies. He felt that these individuals were causing us organizational problems. Another brother mentioned something along the same lines, but added that we need to be quicker in rejecting candidates about whom we have questions. We need to be stricter at the ballot box. Both brothers agreed that Freemasonry has a problem. They also agreed that we need to do something about the problem. I did a lot of thinking about what they both said.

Here's the pressing issue at hand. We are very aware that something is amiss within our ranks. We are eager to rectify it. But how do we go about it? The first step is to step back and view the situation from a different perspective. We must grasp the essence of Freemasonry. It's not a mere civic society or social group. It's a moral philosophy crafted to enhance the quality of life and thinking of its members. If Freemasonry was meant for everyone, we wouldn't need investigation committees or ballot boxes. We'd simply accept new members without much, if any, examination. Even though some lodges seem to follow this approach, we know it's not the right path.

But there is more to this situation. If we reject someone, it is not necessarily a moral judgment. There are many reasons why someone should not be allowed to join Freemasonry that has nothing at all to do with their moral worth. If a man's wife objects to his joining Freemasonry, then he should not be admitted. Moral worth is not the issue. It does not matter how badly the lodge needs new members; Freemasonry is not about causing problems in its members' families. Likewise, if someone believes that Freemasonry is only a club, the investigation committee should correct him on this seriously incorrect belief. If someone with such a belief is not corrected, this is the way that he will view and treat Masonry. If he attends meetings and the lodge is hurting for members, he may soon become Worshipful Master. He will treat the lodge as he understands it. He may then obtain an office in Grand Lodge. He may even become Grand Master. It is certainly not at all impossible. He will still view Freemasonry as another civic group, and that is how he will define it and use his influence to shape it. The whole of Freemasonry will suffer.

So, what do we do?

The failure was on several levels. In too many cases, our investigation committees seem to almost rubber-stamp candidates. They do little more than verify the candidate's name and address. Many jurisdictions now use a third-party paid investigation service that will run a simple background check on the candidates to see if any red flags pop up. Too often, we hear stories of how some candidates joined only to later learn that the investigation service missed something in their background. All blame is placed on the investigation service, but none is placed on the investigation committee. Where were *they*? Why didn't *they* do a proper job of investigating the candidate? The investigation committees are not relieved of their responsibilities just because a Grand Lodge requires lodges to use paid investigation services.

One possible explanation is that the investigation committee was never trained. Untrained investigation committees may exist because the Worshipful Masters were unaware of the training requirements—possibly due to their own lack of training. They advanced through the chairs quickly because there were so few in lodge. In fact, they may be the guys who joined thinking Freemasonry is only another club. The first line of defense for a lodge is any member who signs the petition for membership. No one should sign a petition for someone unknown to them. But once the petition reaches the lodge, it is time for the investigation committee. If they fail in their duty, or if some members question whether the committee is doing a proper job, should we simply blackball the candidate?

If we reject a candidate because we're unsure about our own investigation committee's competence, then the entire lodge has failed. It's a clear indication that we not only consider the candidate unworthy, but also the investigation committee. We seem to be implying that their assessment of the candidate is invalid, and that we know better than they do. If that's the case, then why do we need an investigation committee at all? If we're aware that unworthy individuals have infiltrated our ranks, and if we can't rely on the fairness or accuracy of our own investigation committees, then what's the point of *our* actions? At some point, we need to pause and reconsider the entire situation.

I firmly believe that in all aspects of Freemasonry, the lesson of Hiram holds more significance than we often acknowledge. In the Hiramic lesson, we learn about an unwavering and uncompromising integrity. Put yourself in his shoes. He made an incredibly tough decision. At any point, he could have chosen the easier path and made his personal situation significantly simpler. He could have said, "Oh, this is what you want? Okay, here you go." But he didn't. He refused their demands because he had integrity.

Sometimes being a Mason means that we must make tough decisions and do things that are far from easy. If we have integrity and seek to do what is responsible, then we will try to find a way to do what we know to be right — even if it is terribly difficult. Step back for a moment. We know many have already joined Freemasonry who should never have joined. This does not necessarily mean that they are bad or immoral people. It simply means that either Freemasonry was not adequately explained to them, or the investigation committee failed to do its job due to carelessness or concern over dwindling membership. Regardless of how they accomplished it, they did join us. You can't just throw them out. But it does present problems. We must act responsibly. We must always, *always* hold everyone accountable for their actions. We must put the best interests of the lodge and Masonry first. I don't mean selectively pick and choose who should be held accountable; I mean everyone should be held accountable by the same standard.

Some time back, I remember a lodge that had a truly awful Worshipful Master. He was not only unable to do any of the ritual work. He was unorganized, sloppy-looking, often missed lodge meetings, arrived late when he did, and was generally incompetent. But do you know what? He was a nice guy. After his year was over, a Past Master of the lodge was talking with me about the problems in the lodge. I mentioned the situation with this Master. I told him that it was unfair to the brother as well as to the lodge to have elected him as Master. The brother told me that he disagreed because he felt that *everyone* deserves the chance to be Worshipful Master. I gave a lot of thought to that opinion and realized that this is the club mentality. If we are a club, and nothing that we do really matters, then yes, anyone can be Master, and everyone who joins and shows up should be given this position — especially if the lodge has trouble filling the chairs. Are we a club, or are we something much more? If we are something much more, exactly what are we?

If Masonry is a system of moral and philosophical education, then we must realize that this type of educational system requires specific training. I am neither a medical doctor nor a car mechanic. Sure, I can put Band-Aids on minor injuries, but that's about it. Who in their right mind would come to me to diagnose a serious medical condition *or* a serious auto repair situation? If I am up-front and honest concerning my clear limitations, then anyone who would seek such advice from me would be displaying very poor judgment. I may be the nicest guy in the world, but if you are sick, then you need to see a doctor. If you know that your lodge is not doing well, then putting someone into office only because he is a nice guy, or maybe you feel loyal to him for showing up, makes *you* part of the problem.

If we acknowledge that Freemasonry is not a club, then we are forced to see it for what it is: a complex philosophical education system. This is what we are ... or, we are a club. Which is it? If we are a club, then we need no training, no expectations, and no accountability. We just eat, read minutes, and visit with our friends. If we recognize that we are something much more, and we care about Freemasonry, then we need to look at our present situation and rethink our priorities.

I don't believe that we should blackball candidates who have been approved by an investigation committee (except in extraordinary situations). If the candidate does not live up to what we believe a Mason should be, then we should never again appoint the members of his investigation committee to another such committee. If the new member does not live up to his expectations, then he should not serve in any office. If we don't have enough qualified members to fill the chairs, then we need to close shop. Don't want to close shop? Then make sure that all who serve are qualified to serve. We are who we claim to be, or we are not.

The Minutes

I'd like to discuss a familiar activity in most U.S. lodges — reading the Minutes. Recently, a brother told me of an encounter that he had with a Mason who told him that reading the Minutes was indeed an important part of the *total classic Masonic lodge experience*. This is a good example of how we can take something and twist it up just a little bit so that, in time, it can be completely misunderstood. Let me explain.

I'd like to look at the reading of the Minutes from a little different perspective. I don't want to look at the question (right now) of whether it should be done, but why it may have originally been done. I'd also like to look at the importance of the Minutes themselves.

So, let's start with the question: Are the Minutes important? I guess the answer would be that it depends on whether the Minutes are properly written or not. Accurately taken Minutes provide a record of the activity of the lodge for historical purposes. The Minutes should include which officers are present, the date and time that the lodge opened, and the time that it closed.

The Minutes do not need to be a word-for-word transcription of what was said during the meeting (except for special occasions), but they should include what happened. For example, if someone makes a motion to buy a new air-conditioning unit for the lodge, the exact words of what was said don't have to be recorded. It is important, however, that the general intent be recorded.

If Brother Frank Jones makes a motion to buy a new air-conditioning unit, then that's what should be recorded. If Brother James Smith seconds the motion, that information should be recorded. If several brothers speak in favor of the motion, that information should also be recorded along with their names. If several speak against it, then that should be recorded. The outcome of the vote should be recorded.

The Minutes preserve what happened for the future. Let's say a few years down the line, the air-conditioning unit breaks. All that the members will need to do is to review the Minutes from the vote to purchase the unit for the necessary information regarding the purchase details and the discussion on the subject.

The Minutes should record everything that takes place in the lodge. Proper titles should always be used for all the members, and a general, detailed account of the events taking place in the lodge should be recorded. The reading of the Minutes of the previous lodge meeting is a means of verifying the secretary's performance to ensure he fulfills his duties properly. Of course, it's only a responsible system of checks and balances and not any attempt at casting doubt on the ability or performance of the secretary. This would be the same idea as a yearly audit of the books. It's only something that is done because we are responsible. We check for errors, but we don't check because we assume that errors exist.

The reading of the Minutes ensures that important matters are handled properly. And while it should not have to be said, the reading of the Minutes has no ritualistic or symbolic value. It does not advance the Masonic education of any of the members. It is done solely to ensure that the archives of the lodge contain accurate and complete information. Of course, over time, reading the Minutes has become a routine task that is always done after a lodge is opened. Because it is something that is "always done," we need to be careful that it does not become confused with ritual.

Also, if we are honest with ourselves, many of us tune out during the reading of the Minutes. If we were at the last meeting, we would know what happened. Sure, every now and then someone may offer a correction for something, but generally we just sit there and listen to the Minutes ... or check our email on our phone.

If the secretary keeps less detailed Minutes, then it just means that we will have to endure the process for less time. No matter if we admit it or not, many of the members are a little relieved if the Minutes are kept short and not dragged out. Rarely does anyone consider the historical significance of the Minutes or their importance to the lodge's future. It's just something that must be done and endured. One interesting comment that I heard recently was in support of reading the Minutes in lodge. The Brother said that sitting there and listening to the Minutes is the "least that we can do for our lodge." What?? Does he mean that it is something like an elderly aunt telling us the old story she has told us 100 times before? We sit there and dutifully listen to her because she is family and she is, well ... old. It has no deeper meaning or point. I disagree wholly with this sort of self-punishment. No aspect of Freemasonry should be a bitter pill we force ourselves to swallow, even if it doesn't help us, and we have no idea why we do it. Moral education is not the point or goal of reading the Minutes. Making sure that the Minutes are correct is the goal.

For any Masonic historian or researcher, old Minutes from a lodge are extremely important. From these Minutes, we can learn what happened during any important time. The more detailed the Minutes, the more information we can learn. Sure, if something happened a few years ago, we can ask those members who were present and get a firsthand account that will likely give more information than is contained in the Minutes. But if you are talking about something that happened 50, 100, or 150 years ago, then the Minutes of the lodge will likely be the only place that we can learn about the event. If the Minutes are sloppy or incomplete, then that is all we will have as a historical account of the meeting.

From a historical standpoint, a good secretary provides an extraordinarily important service to the lodge by keeping detailed Minutes. From a practical perspective, a secretary who today keeps the Minutes as bare-bones and basic as possible pleases most of the membership by not forcing them to endure a long reading of the Minutes.

Do you see the problem and the conflict?

Because most members today do not want to listen to a secretary drone on with a lengthy reading of detailed Minutes, the Minutes are kept short and basic. Only what is necessary is often recorded. It is doubtful that any thought is given to the historical aspect of the Minutes and their potential value 100 or 200 years from today.

If the practice of keeping Minutes is to provide a detailed historical account of what took place during a lodge meeting, and if the practice of reading the Minutes was initially designed to be a means of checking the accuracy of the Minutes, then we are today shooting ourselves in the foot. It's time we stopped and gave serious consideration to what we're doing and why. If we don't care and we just want to keep everything as it has been with no thought about why we're doing something, then we are contributing to our own failure.

The Minutes are vitally crucial to the lodge. The Minutes don't have to be read so that everyone can listen to a recap of what took place at the last meeting, but it is very important to make sure that we have a proper historical record of the meeting.

More lodges today are realizing that the reading of the Minutes takes up time that could be spent on Masonic education. They also recognize that printing and placing copies of the Minutes on the secretary's desk provides an opportunity to verify their accuracy without taking up time during the meeting. But there are often objections to not reading the Minutes and only leaving printed copies to be reviewed. Why? Why are there objections?

Well, we often hear objections to doing away with the reading of the Minutes because we are creatures of habit. For as long as any of us have been Masons, the Minutes have been read out. No other reason. No real thought is given to why the Minutes are read, only that they are read and have been read for a very long time, so we should continue to do it.

The benefit of printing copies of the Minutes is twofold: it saves time by eliminating the need to read them aloud, and it allows the secretary to provide more detailed Minutes without overwhelming the members with a lengthy recap of the previous meeting.

We must understand that the goal of having Minutes is to provide as detailed a record as possible of each lodge meeting. It is not the act of reading the Minutes aloud that is important. It is making sure that the Minutes are accurate and complete. We must understand that when lodges began reading the Minutes, it was done at that time because they did not have computers or photo-copy machines. They *had* to read the Minutes aloud if they wanted the members to have the opportunity to verify their accuracy. That's all that they could reasonably do. They did their best.

The secretary should make as detailed a record as possible of each lodge meeting. That is his job and what every responsible secretary will do. To prove that this job is properly done, the secretary provides those Minutes to the lodge for examination at the next meeting. That is his responsibility. It is the responsibility of the members to verify what he offers to make sure that all is correct. If either side fails to fulfill its duties, the lodge loses.

Lodges use electric lights because they are available. Lodges use air-conditioning units and heaters because they are available. We understand that 150 years ago, lodges did not have either electric lights or air-conditioning units. We know they did the best they could with what they had. We use modern conveniences because we have them, and it's the smart thing to do.

150 years ago, lodge secretaries read out the Minutes because that was the only way that they could reasonably provide the information to the lodge without handwriting a whole stack of Minutes. Today, we can do far better. We can use our computers to print copies of the Minutes to be given to the members rather than wasting time on reading the Minutes out loud. We can use the time that is saved by doing what we should be doing — Masonic education. We are Masons; we teach moral improvement. The lesson of the Beehive is not to teach us busy work. It is to keep doing what is most useful for the whole.

Of course, if, regardless of everything else, it remains our desire to have our meetings consist only of the secretary reading the abbreviated Minutes along with bills and reports of who is sick or has died, then we can do that. If we want to bore and run off many of our new members by giving them pointless, empty work in place of Masonic education, I guess that is our right. Maybe we should give up our electric lights and central air units as well. It makes as much sense.

MASONIC JURISPRUDENCE

Masonic law, or its philosophical counterpart, Masonic jurisprudence, serves as a guiding light, defining what is proper or improper in Masonry. It provides a framework for the operation of a lodge and the conduct of individual Masons, both within and outside the lodge, offering a sense of direction and support.

Masonic law not only governs our conduct within the lodge but also shapes our relationships with the Grand Lodge, our own lodge, individual Masons, and even non-Masons. It fosters a sense of connection and responsibility, guiding our interactions in general society.

It is indispensable for all Masons to be familiar with their lodge bylaws and the Grand Lodge handbook of Masonic law, or the publication that outlines the rules and regulations of their Grand Lodge. With this basic information, we can navigate the proper operation of the lodge and conduct ourselves in a manner in accordance with Freemasonry as practiced in most jurisdictions.

Because each jurisdiction is sovereign and independent, Masonic law varies from jurisdiction to jurisdiction. However, the Grand Lodge, the highest governing body in Freemasonry, plays a crucial role in setting and interpreting these laws. While there are a good number of generally accepted procedures that will be used by many to most jurisdictions, it is dangerous to represent *anything* as the law of *all* Masonry. The final authority on any rule, regulation, or law of Masonry is your own Grand Lodge. The only thing that I will say in this paper that definitely applies to everyone is that you should read, learn, and follow the rules and regulations of your Grand Lodge.

The first aspect of lodge operation and law that I would like to talk about is a procedure that we have all gone through prior to joining Masonry. This would be the process from the investigation committee to the ballot box (See the chapter on the Ballot Box for more information).

The actions of an investigation committee, as well as those who ballot on a candidate, are profound and sobering. They are entrusted with the responsibility of evaluating the worthiness of another human being, a task that empowers them with a sense of responsibility and respect for Masonic values. Any thinking person will realize what a tremendous and awesome responsibility is placed upon us. I can think of no way to disrespect Masonry greater than an investigation committee that is lax or negligent in their duties.

And now we come to the ballot box. There is no greater test of the integrity of a Mason and no greater trust *in* that integrity than with the ballot box. I don't believe any instruction on how to use the ballot box is necessary here, as it certainly has been explained to all Masons in their lodge. But I will point out that *because* the balloting is done in secret, at least in all jurisdictions of which I am familiar, a special trust is displayed. The lodge places complete confidence in the integrity of all Masons that they will ballot in the best interest of Freemasonry and with the honor expected of Freemasons.

When we look at a Masonic lodge, the one officer that truly stands out and is unique in the world of organizations and clubs is the office of Worshipful Master. The authority given to the Master of a lodge far exceeds the authority given to the presiding officer of any club. This is one of the reasons why the standard edition of *Roberts Rules of Order* is so problematic when used in a lodge. It is also why some years back; I revised the work into a Masonic Edition[1] to make it more suitable for use in the lodge.

To give just one example, in a club, if the presiding officer rules something out of order, members of the club can call for a vote in an effort to overturn the ruling. If it is overturned, then the ruling of the presiding officer becomes invalid. No such provision exists in Freemasonry. If the Master rules something out of order, that ruling is final. There is no recourse in the lodge for such a ruling. The idea that Freemasonry is a true democracy is just not correct. If the Master were to make some grievous error or abuse of his authority, then the only recourse would be through the Grand Lodge. In a lodge setting the decision of the Master is final.

But there are limits to the authority of the Worshipful Master.

The Master does not have the authority to overrule the vote of a lodge. If the Master believes that a motion is out of order, then he can rule it as such and refuse the call for a vote. But if he does call for a vote, then he also becomes bound to the vote of the lodge. Once the lodge has voted his hands are tied. The duties and prerogatives of a Worshipful Master are typically spelled out in Grand Lodge monitors or books of law.

The rules, laws, duties, and prerogatives of a Worshipful Master for your jurisdiction should be read and studied carefully by anyone seeking to work through the chairs of a lodge.

Another area of Masonic law that is always painful is a Masonic trial. Because Masons are human, we sometimes fail and can violate the trust a lodge has placed in us.

Each Grand Lodge has rules and regulations concerning Masonic trials. If there is ever a concern that someone has committed a Masonic offense and the possibility of a Masonic trial exists, then you should seek the advice of knowledgeable Masons. The

Master or Secretary of the lodge should be contacted, and, if necessary, contact a District Deputy Grand Master or the office of the Grand Secretary.

A Masonic trial is, without question, nothing that should be taken lightly. You should never threaten a Masonic trial during an argument with a brother, nor make bluffs about filing charges on another Mason. If someone has committed an offense serious enough for Masonic trial, then you should begin the process. Don't threaten, just do it. But you should *never* file Masonic charges if no real offense has taken place. You should, however, file Masonic charges if an actual offense has taken place. Not filing Masonic charges, when they *are* warranted, is as bad as filing them when it is not warranted.

But when is something an actual Masonic offense?

In all cases, and this cannot be said enough, *seek the counsel of knowledgeable Masons*. Do not do anything if you are angry or upset. Do not do anything unless you are very sure. Know what the Masonic law is and be sure of every step you take.

If you believe an individual Mason or Grand Lodge officer has committed an unjust action, *never, never, never* take your grievances and publicly air them with names and actual cases on social media or any other public platform. Making a public spectacle of perceived flaws in specific Masons or Masonic organizations is the definition of speaking evil. This is *not* how worthy Masons act or solve problems. Any Mason using public soapbox tactics to call attention to perceived flaws in individual Masons or Masonic bodies should be ignored and recognized as unMasonic in their actions.

Suppose you have the unfortunate responsibility of holding office in a lodge during a Masonic trial. In that case, you are to pay close attention to your Masonic handbook of law to make sure that everything is done properly. The Master and Secretary of the lodge should maintain close contact with the Grand Secretary's office to ensure they are following all rules and regulations of your jurisdiction.

In the case of a Masonic trial, there is no single rule that applies universally, as each jurisdiction has its own rules and guidelines for proper conduct. Even if a lodge has never conducted a Masonic trial before, the possibility always exists.

Those seeking to become Worshipful Master of the lodge should learn and be familiar with how to conduct a trial in the event it occurs. A Masonic trial is not something that an inexperienced or poorly qualified Master would want to tackle on his own. Seek help, seek guidance, do not act without advice.

Aristotle is said to have written, "At his best, man is the noblest of all animals; separated from law and justice he is the worst." I believe that this is exactly why Masonry was created around the concept of very specific rules and laws.

Our obligations are laws, and we agreed to bind ourselves to them under penalty of trial and possible expulsion. We are expected to obey the laws of the land, yet we can be put on trial for violations of laws that are not found in any criminal code or general societal lawbook. We are held to a higher standard. Why? It is because far more is expected from those who are given far more.

Masonry, I believe, has a vulnerability that stems from the way we perceive ourselves, the trust we have in our brothers, and the manner in which we formulate our laws. We don't expect our brothers to be anything but noble.

As a boy, I remember my grandfather, a Past Master, telling me that he would trust a Mason with anything he had. He said that he would trust a Mason he didn't know in his home alone with all his valuables around. He said that he would trust him *because* he was a Mason. Just a few years ago, I asked a Mason if he would do as my grandfather had done. He smiled and said that there was no way that he would trust *anyone* he didn't know in his home alone with his valuables. Who is right and who is wrong?

Being a Mason meant something to my grandfather. But what did it mean to him? What does it mean to Masons today? Are we without Masonic law and justice? Is *Masonic jurisprudence* merely a set of words that we say without understanding? Maybe to some.

I have seen a new wave of Masons who seek the deeper aspects of Freemasonry. I see young Masons who want the social clubs to be replaced with authentic Masonic lodges. To be so, we need to be noble. We need to know what a "true Masonic lodge" and a "true Mason" means. We need fair and firm laws, rules, and regulations with which to govern our lodges. We need to have the integrity to uphold our laws and the strength to ensure that everyone does the same.

My grandfather also told me one other thing. He said that if Masonry were easy, everyone would be a Mason. He was right.

Notes

1. Poll, Michael R., Rev. *Robert's Rules of Order: Masonic Edition*. New Orleans, LA: Cornerstone Book Publishers, 2005.

WHEN WE STRAY

Not long ago, I was going through some boxes in storage and stumbled upon one I hadn't seen in years. It contained personal items from around the time that I joined Masonry. One of the things that I found was a small booklet my lodge had printed just after I had joined. It was the lodge bylaws and roster of members.

As I pored over the booklet, the names of members long gone stirred memories of the events and conversations from that time. I vividly recall a conversation with an elderly Mason who fascinated me with tales of how Masons would support each other during the most challenging times in our history, such as the Great Depression of the late 1920s and 30s, or during WWII in the US. These stories underscore the profound historical significance of Masonic conduct, instilling in us a deep reverence for our tradition.

He recounted the great shortages of items like sugar and coffee, and the rationing that was in place. Ration coupons were distributed, and once they were used up, one had to go without. Even seemingly trivial items like white dress shirts, commonly worn to lodge, were rationed. He also shared instances where some Masons exploited their Masonic identity to bend the rules.

Masons would sometimes wear their Masonic ring turned around so that the S&C would face their palm and go into a store or shop that they knew was run by a Mason. They would then ask for an item that required a coupon. When asked for the coupon, the Mason would not say a word, but instead of giving the coupon, he would turn his ring around to its proper position, placing his hand down on the counter so that the shop owner could see the ring. Not a word was spoken, but the sale was made without the coupon. It was a challenging time.

Things like showing a Masonic ring may have been done out of a feeling that Masons should help each other. But when does it go too far?

I recall the guidelines set by my Grand Lodge regarding the association of Masonry with any business. It was deemed unethical for a Mason to use the S&C on any business card or advertisement. This was seen as an improper use of Masonry, with the underlying motive being personal gain.

It was the same to link any Masonic symbol, lodge name, or any aspect of Masonry to a business. Of course, I've seen some lodge rosters from the early to mid-1800s that not only gave the name and address of each member, but also listed his occupation, or place of employment. Is this information solely about the member, a subtle advertisement, or perhaps a blend of both? It's hard to tell.

Another area of interest is Masons in politics. Now, for as long as Masonry has existed, some Masons have served in political offices. Many Masonic history books clearly brag on the U.S. presidents who have been Masons, yet discussion of both religion and politics is forbidden in lodges at labor. So, if someone is running for a political office, where is the line not to cross between Masonic information and using Masonry for personal gain? I'm not sure that there is a clear line anymore — or maybe if there ever were clear lines. If someone said in a political speech, "Vote for me because I am a Freemason!" then I am sure most would agree that this has crossed the line.

But is it crossing the line to list Masonic Membership among the organizations to which a candidate belongs? I remember not very long ago, a website came under severe criticism because it listed the names of Masons and their places of employment. It was a Masonic directory where Masons could list their names and places of employment for free. There were no lines of promotion for the businesses; instead, it was noted that this was where the Masons worked. A few Grand Lodges warned their members that if they listed themselves on this site, they could face Masonic discipline.

Today, I've noticed that some Grand Lodge websites have similar Masonic directories. It seems that times and attitudes have changed, leading to a more relaxed approach towards the public display of Masonic membership.

When I first joined Masonry, one of my early mentors was an attorney by profession. He was well respected, but his business card was as basic as it could be. It was a white card with black ink and only contained his name, address, phone number, and the single line below his name: "Attorney at Law." He was aghast at some of the simple TV commercials from attorneys advertising their services. He told me that this was *highly* improper and did not know why the ethics board did not act on them.

He has long gone to his reward, but I sometimes wonder how he would react to some of the TV commercials from many of today's attorneys. Times do change, and with them, some attitudes change. So again, where is the line that Masons should not cross?

When are we providing simple, general information on ourselves, and when are we using Masonic membership for improper personal gain? The answer might be subjective. When is someone telling a joke, and when are they making fun of you?

Usually, if something doesn't feel right, it is not right. But, then again, everyone has their own moral compass.

The reason we have a Masonic trial is that some Masons believe they can act as they see fit, even if it contradicts the views of most other Masons. I don't think that I can give a definitive answer. And, even if I could give a definitive answer for today, there is no guarantee that it would be valid tomorrow. Then again, even if my jurisdiction has a firm position, that does not mean it is the accepted position in other jurisdictions.

The best answer may exist within our Masonic teachings. There are times when we need to do the hard things. When we serve on an investigation committee, we are charged with admitting only those we deem to be morally worthy. But what does that mean? How do you know someone else's heart? Should we be kind-hearted and let everyone in? If we do that, then why do we need an investigation committee to begin with?

Freemasonry is not for everyone. To believe it is, is to misunderstand the nature and purpose of Freemasonry. Freemasonry is not designed to be an insurance agency where its members pay dues with the expected goal of reaping financial benefits at some point.

It is also not an association where its members use their membership to gain an unfair advantage over non-Masons in business or general society. We should be better than engaging in such activity. So, where is the line that we should not cross? How do we know when we or someone else has entered an area that is improper for Masons to travel?

The first place that I would suggest looking for such answers is in your Masonic law book. The answer may be right there in black and white. If you have difficulty in finding the answer, ask someone in your lodge or Grand Lodge. They may be able to point you in the right direction. If there is still no completely clear answer, then you may need to find your answers in our teachings. Pick up a book on Freemasonry. Read it. Then pick up and read another, then another. Don't stop. Seek and keep seeking, studying, and learning Freemasonry. This is where you will find your answers.

If your Freemasonry is only a club for fellowship, you simply will never find the answers you may (or may not) seek. But on the other hand, you may find that the answer has always been inside you and it is the answer that feels right and seems in your heart to be the obvious answer. Does this seem vague? Maybe it is, but the voice inside us is often soft. We just may need to pay more attention to what we truly already know.

IRREGULARITY

Not long ago I received an email from a new Mason. He said that he met a Mason who identified himself as a 33rd degree Scottish Rite Mason. He then added that the Mason belonged to a jurisdiction not recognized by his jurisdiction. He wanted to know how he should treat him.

The Brother was serious, and it was clear that this situation had never been mentioned to him by any of the members of his lodge or his Scottish Rite Valley. He honestly did not know how to treat someone from an unrecognized jurisdiction. Let's look at this question.

First off, Grand Lodges maintain what's known as "Fraternal Relations" with other Masonic bodies, or they don't. This means that all the lodges under any jurisdiction that has Fraternal Relations with your Grand Lodge are usually OK to visit. If Fraternal Relations do not exist, then visitation or discussion of things that should be reserved for a lodge at labor are usually not allowed. But it needs to be pointed out that each jurisdiction has its own rules. For more specific information as to the rules and regulations concerning visitation for you, I strongly suggest you contact your Grand Secretary's office.

But the problem that I sometimes see is Masons who get carried away with things. Some feel that if Fraternal Relations do not exist with another body, then it means that they have a right, or maybe even a duty, to be rude or unpleasant to the other person. In my opinion, this type of attitude is unMasonic and contrary to everything that we teach in Freemasonry.

We must obey the laws, rules, and regulations of our own jurisdiction, but at the same time we are not to be discourteous to others simply because they may belong to a jurisdiction that we don't today recognize. Lack of Fraternal Relations does not automatically mean irregularity. And even if someone is not considered today as a regular Mason, or not a Mason at all, it doesn't mean that they are not a good human being. A Mason is not a superior being simply by possessing regular Masonic membership. Our value as a human depends on our conduct and actions.

Let's look for a minute at Freemasonry in the United States. There are, for the most part, two types of recognized Freemasonry. That would be what's known as "mainstream" Masonry and Prince Hall Masonry.

Mainstream Masonry is normally the older Masonry and sometimes called the "white Grand Lodge." This is because there was a time in the history of US Freemasonry when if you were not white, you were not allowed to become a Mason. It was truly an unenlightened time.

Prince Hall Masonry was created to give African-Americans the same opportunity to join Freemasonry as those who happened to be born white. There was also a very interesting rule that became agreed upon in the very early days of Masonry in the United States. That rule was that there could only be one Grand Lodge per state. With that rule, any additional Grand Lodge became automatically irregular. You will find that in many cases, rules determine regularity rather than living the Masonic philosophy.

So, from its very early days in the late 1700s, Prince Hall Masonry was deemed to be irregular because it was technically an additional Grand Lodge, and it violated the rules. But, in reality, it was simply because its members were not white. Fraternal Relations did not exist between any Grand Lodge in the United States and its Prince Hall counterpart for nearly 200 years.

Over time, the idea that a Mason needed to be white was recognized as ignorant, hateful, and wholly unMasonic in most all jurisdictions. New Masons were made in "Mainstream" jurisdictions regardless of race. But Prince Hall Masonry was still considered outside of regular Freemasonry.

Everything changed in 1989 with the recognition of the Prince Hall Grand Lodge of Connecticut by the Grand Lodge of Connecticut. But there still existed that rule about only one Grand Lodge being allowed in a state. So, what did they do? A few Grand Lodges broke Fraternal Relations for a short time with the Grand Lodge of Connecticut. But they soon realized that this was not the right path. Their answer was to modify that troublesome rule.

The new understanding of the rule of Exclusive Territorial Jurisdiction became one Grand Lodge per state unless the Grand Lodge decides to enter into fraternal relations with another Grand Lodge in the same state. With that modification of the rule, we have today most US Grand lodges enjoying fraternal relations with their Prince Hall Masonic counterparts.

But think about exactly what it meant when a Grand Lodge recognized (entered into Fraternal Relations) with its Prince Hall counterpart. Prior to a Grand Lodge and its Prince Hall counterpart entering into Fraternal Relations, did they view each other as regular? In many Grand Lodge proceedings, you'll find Prince Hall Masonry being defined as irregular. It was not until Fraternal Relations were established did they begin to call each other regular. Why? Did something change in the nature of either Grand Lodge that caused them to be viewed as regular? No. In all cases, the only thing that changed was that fraternal relations were established.

Freemasonry in the United States seemed to link the existence of Fraternal Relations with regularity and the lack of Fraternal

Relations with irregularity. Once Fraternal Relations started happening between US Grand Lodges and their Prince Hall counterparts the definition of regularity changed.

But regularity must mean something apart from just the existence of Fraternal Relations. Regularity cannot be only automatically tied to, or understood as, the existence of Fraternal Relations. If we do so, then the recognition between US Grand lodges and their Prince Hall counterparts makes no sense at all.

Yes, there are established rules about regularity of origin, regularity of work and so on. But, so very much about regularity seems completely subjective.

Nothing about the nature of Prince Hall Masonry changed prior to or after its recognition. Prince Hall Masonry was, and is, regular Masonry that was just not recognized as such for many years — or it was never regular. This does not mean that every single organization that calls itself Masonic is regular by how we normally define regular. But it also does not mean that regularity is determined *only* by the existence of Fraternal Relations.

This brings us to another point.

I have seen some Masonic bodies that truthfully have no legitimate claim to regularity by how Freemasonry determines regularity. (And for how Freemasonry determines regularity, see your Grand Secretary's office for the particular details for your own jurisdiction.) However, some of the Masons who belong to some of these irregular bodies sure act like regular Freemasons.

How can we explain that?

Well, Freemasonry is all about an individual following a certain set of teachings in order to improve himself. These teachings are not secret. Our teachings are right there for the world to see.

So, if according to the rules of Freemasonry, some Grand Lodges are, after examination, determined to not be regular for some technical reason, does that mean that it's impossible for its members to benefit from the Masonic teachings? I don't believe that's true at all. Also, is it possible for regular Masons to benefit from the teachings of an irregular Mason? Think about that question for a while.

If you pick up any book or list of famous Masons, you will find Benjamin Franklin's name included. This highly respected scientist, journalist, inventor, statesman, and one of the Founding Fathers of the United States was also a devoted Freemason, and even Grand Master. In 1734, Franklin edited and published the first Masonic book in the American colonies, a reprint of James Anderson's Constitutions of the Free-Masons. What might not be usually understood is that in the eyes of the United States Masonic community at that time, Benjamin Franklin was viewed as an irregular Master Mason. That's right. He belonged to a Grand Lodge that for technical reasons was not, at that time, recognized as regular.[1] And yet we claim him as a famous Freemason who is worthy of emulation — and he was!

And, what about this 33rd degree Mason that the young brother wrote to me about? Should we disregard all 33rds who belong to a body that may not be viewed, for some reason, as regular? Well, I should point out that John Mitchell, 33rd died as an irregular Master Mason. Who was John Mitchell? Well, he was the first Sovereign Grand Commander of the Supreme Council Southern Jurisdiction, USA. That's the Mother Supreme Council of the World — the first Grand Commander of the first Scottish Rite Supreme Council. Yep, in the eyes of the U.S. Masonic community of that time, John Mitchell died as an irregular Master Mason.[2]

Of course, John Mitchell was not always viewed as an irregular Master Mason, but he became irregular because of technicalities regarding that old concept of only one recognized Grand Lodge per state.[3] So exactly what does regularity mean and how much stock can we place in it when we look at an individual Mason?

As I've mentioned before, Freemasonry is of a dual nature. We have both the Masonic philosophy and the Masonic organization.

Each organization of Freemasonry, and that includes each Grand Lodge, has its own rules and regulations. The choice for the members is to obey the rules of their organization or not be a member. It's as simple as that.

When new Masons are not properly taught the rules and regulations of their jurisdictions, problems can and do develop. Visitation and who can and who cannot visit is often not properly taught to new Masons. This is why I advise over and over again that if anyone has questions about what is or is not proper in their jurisdiction do not go online and try to find out for yourself. You can ask a question and receive a completely correct answer for another jurisdiction that is completely wrong for your own jurisdiction. The best place to learn about your jurisdiction is your own Worshipful Master, educated members, your District Deputy Grand Master, or your Grand Secretary.

But again, we are talking about the organization of Freemasonry. The philosophy is different. Our philosophy is designed to help the individual improve himself. That's it. We also don't say how much, we don't say how little, and we don't say exactly how. We simply provide all Masons with teachings and symbolic instructions on how anyone who applies these teachings can live a better life.

The level of benefit from our teachings to the individual depends on the level of work they put into learning and living the lessons. These teachings are also not part of our secret instruction. The only common thing that's secret in Masonry are matters of recognition and initiation. All lessons to help improve our members are open and free to anyone.

So, if our goal is ultimately to make ourselves better, and we make the instruction of how to do this available to anyone, then we are in fact benefiting members of our organization as well as those who are not members but choose to take advantage of what we teach. This brings us to what may seem like very strange situations concerning the members of our organization. This is especially true if members of our organization *do not* take advantage of our teachings, and yet others who are not members *do* take advantage of what we offer.

So, who is the real Mason, a member of our organization who knows nothing about our teachings, or the nonmember or even the so-called irregular Mason who has taken the time to learn and benefit from what we teach? The members of our organization have dues cards. But there is no guarantee that they have benefited from, or even know much about, what we teach. The Master Mason or even the 33rd degree Mason may or may not know any more about the deeper Masonic philosophy than the average guy on the street.

On the other hand, one who belongs to an irregular lodge of Masons may truly walk in the philosophy of what we teach. This places us in an interesting position. What does it mean to be a Mason? Are we a Mason if we possess a dues card? Are we a Mason if we live and practice the teachings of Freemasonry?

All new candidates are asked where they were first prepared to be made a Mason. The answer is in the heart. When these individuals were first prepared to be made a Mason, they did not have a dues card. They were not members of our organization. I believe that in all things in life we must seek a balance and that sometimes (maybe more times than we realize) to grow we have to adjust how we think.

The organization of Freemasonry is limited to those who are members. The philosophy of Freemasonry is limited to those who take the time to study the Masonic teachings. There is no requirement for members of the organization to understand its philosophy. There is no prohibition for those who are not members of our organization to study and benefit from our philosophy. It is my opinion that those who are not members of our organization and yet take the time to study our philosophy and know our teachings are truly special human beings.

Those members of our organization who act superior to anyone else simply by virtue of their membership in our organization, or by any office they have held, or any degree that they have received, display a particularly profound failure in the understanding of exactly what it is that we teach. Their Masonic foundation is built on the unsteady sand of ego.

Because of the rules, regulations, and laws of our organization we have limits on how we can interact with those who are not members of our own organization. But if we have any understanding of what we teach, then we must treat all Seekers of Light with the respect due those souls who understand and live by the Masonic Light.

We must acknowledge kindred spirits, maybe not through the limitations of organizational rules, but with the unlimited respect and admiration of those who truly walk the path that we should all walk. In other words, be nice, don't judge, respect kindred spirits, and act as a true Mason.

We are, and can be, so much more than just a dues card or a certificate with our name on it.

Notes

1. *Proceedings of the Most Worshipful Grand Lodge of Ancient Free and Accepted Masons of the Commonwealth of Massachusetts for the Year 1914.* Poole Printing Company Boston 1915 pp 251-253.

2. Michael R. Poll, *The Scottish Rite Papers*, (New Orleans, LA: Cornerstone Book Publishers, 2020) pp 1-21.

3. Ibid.

ANTI-MASONRY

Some years back, a Mason told me of an encounter that he had with an anti-Mason. Although he was not a new Mason, he was still shocked by the encounter. He had difficulty understanding the logic of the anti-Masons. He told me that he had known the man for many years and considered him a friend, but the subject of Freemasonry had never come up in any of their conversations. When the man learned that he was a Freemason, his entire attitude towards him changed. He then began making charges that the Mason *knew* were not correct. Still, because he was not a student of Masonic history nor was he well read in its philosophy, he was not able to properly defend Masonry from the many charges that the man made. He described it as a helpless feeling, hearing what he knew were false charges being made, yet being unable to mount a proper defense.

The fact is that anti-Masonry has existed for about as long as Freemasonry has existed. There is a thought that for the world to be in proper balance, everything must have an equal opposite. For there to be light, there must be dark; if there is good, there must also be bad, and so on. This is often represented by the black and white mosaic checkerboard floor. It is symbolic of the balance of the universe with a positive/negative, good/evil, light /dark balance represented by the black and white squares on the floor. If

Freemasonry is the pure philosophy that it is represented to be, then we must understand that it must have an opposite negative opponent.

Freemasonry must be challenged and forced to defend itself from the other end of the spectrum if it is to remain a pure philosophy. If this thought is correct, then anti-Masonry is not a phenomenon that needs to be crushed out. Anti-Masonry is very much needed to provide balance to the Masonic philosophy and to remain a constant test to it so that it does not diminish in value.

However, it's crucial to remember that understanding the underlying reasons for anti-Masonry is only part of the solution. The real power to defend Freemasonry lies in our knowledge of it. If we limit our engagement with Freemasonry to business meetings and socializing, we won't be equipped to counter the falsehoods that are often spread about it.

In his paper, *The Rise and Development of Anti-Masonry in America 1737-1826,*[1] J. Hugo Tatsch tells us of an alarming early account of anti-Masonry. He writes of a con man who tricked people into joining what he said was Freemasonry, only to put them through ridiculous and humiliating situations for personal entertainment. The sham rituals ended in tragedy when one candidate was set on fire and died a painful death several days later. Because the man represented what he offered *as Freemasonry*, actual Freemasonry was painted with his brush.

From my perspective, there are three general categories of anti-Masonry. One is a fanatical anti-Masonry, where individuals choose to believe almost anything bad about Masonry simply because someone, usually a man representing himself as a man of the cloth, tells them nonsense is fact. Their belief in terrible things about Masonry becomes almost interwoven into their religious faith.

Another form of anti-Masonry is business anti-Masonry. Some individuals advance all sorts of anti-Masonic activity and teachings, even some in the guise of religion, but the end is always to sell things for personal profit. Since they make a good living off anti-Masonry, they are hardly ready to change their tune.

The third form of anti-Masonry is more complicated. It is when individuals start *what they claim to be* Masonic lodges, identify themselves *as such*, and then deceive those who know no better into joining them. They make their living by *pretending* to be Masonry, yet they offer nothing in the way of Masonry to those who join them. The general public, often knowing little to nothing of Masonry, believes them to be true Masonry, recognizes what they did as a con, and blames Freemasonry itself. The whole of Masonry suffers.

Let's look deeper at these situations.

Back in the 1980s, I had two first-hand accounts of what could be called fanatical anti-Masonry. I remember a woman who was a yoga instructor, and my mother was one of her students. This instructor and my mother became friends, and I remember the instructor coming over to the house often to visit.

At some point thereafter, the yoga instructor joined a church that felt that yoga was an abomination. This church also taught that anyone who belonged to Freemasonry was not only a sinner but also not a Christian, no matter what they believed. Now, I didn't know anything about this, and one day I came into the house to find both of them talking. The woman was telling my mother how she was giving up teaching yoga and the reasons for it. As they were talking, the woman looked up and saw my Masonic ring. Without hardly missing a beat, she looked me right in the eyes and said, "You don't believe in God." I was caught off guard, surprised, and unsure of what to say to the woman.

I simply told her that I did believe in God. She immediately told me that I was wrong. She said that she knew that I did not. I was young at the time and not entirely prepared to deal with something that seems so absurd to me. I couldn't understand how she could believe she had any idea what was in my heart. I asked her how she could believe such a thing about someone she didn't really know. She said that her minister told her. I was even more shocked, still unsure if I was hearing her correctly. I pointed out that this was not a better answer, as her minister had never laid eyes on me. She told me that her minister told her that anyone who does not belong to her church does not believe in God. I was stunned at the total illogic of such an answer. I attributed the problem to her personally, assuming she must be an irrational person (I thought she was nuts). I dismissed the event as just nonsense from a strange woman.

About six months to a year later, a second incident happened. I was working at the time in downtown New Orleans, and parking in that area was very expensive. We had a convenient public transportation system, and I would take the bus to work every day. I would come home every evening at about the same time. As I was walking home, I would pass a neighbor's house who lived down the street from me. Most days, I would see him sitting out in a lawn chair reading his Bible. I didn't really think much of it. I would typically wave at him and ask how he was doing. We didn't get into any long conversations, but the greetings were always friendly. One day, we were exchanging a few words, and he noticed that I was wearing a Masonic ring. His attitude changed a bit, and he asked if I was a Freemason. I told him yes. He then told me that I probably didn't know that this was an evil organization. He said that he had proof that would confirm what he said. He asked if I would wait for a minute, and he would get me this "proof." I knew he was wrong, but I wasn't in the mood to debate him, so I simply told him "No, thanks," dismissed the conversation, and went home.

For about a month or so after, every time that neighbor saw me, he would ask if I could give him a few moments so that he could show me the "proof" that he had on Masonry. He said that he had the documents that would show without question that Freemasonry was Satanic. He said that he cared about me and didn't want me to continue "sinning" by being a member. I usually just waved at him and told him that I didn't have time. Well, one Friday, he caught me in the right mood, and I told him that I would take a look at what he had. He went inside and came back with a briefcase. The briefcase was filled with a large number of photocopies of various documents. He said that this was proof that Freemasonry is evil. I told him that reviewing this many documents at once was too much, and I asked if I could take them home for the weekend to look over. He told me that this was fine, and I went home to look over the material.

When I started looking through the documents in the briefcase, I saw that they were all photocopies from various anti-Masonic books and leaflets. All the copies showed various quotes that seemed to be from Masons. Each of the quotes looked to be properly cited. I have a fairly good Masonic library, and I had a copy of each of the books from where the quotes were taken. Invariably, each and every quote that was cited was either out of context, misquoted, or wholly made up. I recall a quote from a Grand Master's speech: "Masonry is evil, it is satanic." I looked in the book from where the speech was transcribed, and what the Grand Master actually said was, "I would be telling a lie if I said that Masonry is evil, it is satanic." So, I sat down and for each and every quote that he gave, I provided the correction from the original source. It seems that I was naïve because I thought that by providing him with all the corrections, he would change his view of Freemasonry. I fully expected to sit down with him, show him the corrections, and for him to say, "Gee, I guess I was wrong about Freemasonry."

I went back to the man's house and sat down with him. I presented each piece of his evidence, demonstrating how none of them accurately represented what they were claimed to say. There was no debate in the matter; the proof he claimed to show me simply did not exist. When I finished, he didn't say anything; he just sat there. I finally said, "Do you see that the proof you said you were going to show me does not exist?" The man looked me right in the eyes and said, "No, I don't see that at all. Jesus is my proof." I was completely baffled. I grew up as a Christian, but not once had I been taught that Jesus supported falsehoods. He had created a situation where he knowingly and willingly accepted lies, and his only defense was a professed belief that Jesus would agree with supporting falsehoods. I didn't know what to say, so I left.

Someone who I consider to be a religious fanatic is *not* one who simply holds firmly to a religious belief. The very nature of religion means that it goes outside the realm of scientific proof. A religious fanatic will take *an unsanctioned* detail of their religion and then deny truth itself to hold onto that religious modification. An example would be an anti-Mason who holds certain misconceptions about Freemasonry, as my former neighbor did. They will hold onto these misconceptions *as* a religious belief, even when they are proven incorrect.

Another example would be the friend of my mother who claimed to *know the heart* of a stranger. She claimed to *know* the private beliefs of a stranger simply on the suggestion of her minister. The fanatical aspects of these people had *nothing to do* with their belief in a Supreme Being; it had to do with the *judgments* they freely made about other human beings.

There is another type of anti-Masonry that began in the 1990s that created a good bit of excitement in US Masonry. I'm unsure whether this particular anti-Masonic movement *has always* existed in its current form or if it initially took one path and then diverged. In the late 80s and early 90s, there was unrest in the religious organization known as the Southern Baptist Convention. A small group of members began an organized attack on Freemasonry. Their claim was that Freemasonry was incompatible with Christianity. Their support for this claim was exactly the same as the "proof" displayed by my former neighbor — meaning, out-of-context quotes, misquotes, and outright fabricated quotes. The problem for many Masons was that they did not have readily available Masonic reference books and were unable to properly counter the charges made against them.

It was around this time that two of my Masonic friends, Arturo de Hoyos and S. Brent Morris wrote a book titled, *Is it True What They Say About Freemasonry?*[2] Initially, I was critical of this book as I felt that it was improper for Freemasons, *or Freemasonry,* to dignify such irrational attacks with answers. Their talents seemed better suited to other areas of research. I didn't feel it *fitting* for them to try to change the minds of those who didn't want to be changed. *I was wrong.* I considered this movement a fanatical movement. I failed to realize, *at the beginning,* that business played a part in this particular anti-Masonic movement.

The young internet was used successfully by these anti-Masons to spread their Masonic propaganda. Mixed in with their falsehoods was a cleverly disguised sales campaign. We must understand that the libraries possessed by most Masons consist of, at most, a few general Masonic encyclopedias. Most Masons were unable to properly defend and expose the so-called "proof" of these anti-Masons for what it was.

The documents containing misquotes, out-of-context quotes, and outright made-up quotes made impressive-sounding and very believable evidence to those who knew little of Freemasonry. It was not long before books were written *by* these anti-Masons containing this false information. Because of their religious-sounding delivery method and persistence of these anti-Masonic leaders, these books did become popular, and before long, successful anti-Masonic businesses were created.

Grand Lodges had long been lax in maintaining things such as copyrights on their monitors and other printed material. Most Grand Lodges were also more concerned with replenishing dwindling membership than fighting possibly difficult copyright battles with anti-Masons. The result was that monitors and other printed materials were stolen by anti-Masons, who then reprinted them to sell on their websites. These anti-Masons found a good business in selling falsehoods. Believable arguments were made, and it was an attractive sales technique. It was successful.

Around this same time, CompuServe was a popular internet service provider. CompuServe offered community forums on a very wide variety of interests. For those discovering the young internet, the CompuServe forums were fascinating and popular. It was here that one of the very early Masonic forums was created — the CompuServe Masonry Forum. There were also several religion forums on CompuServe, and these were soon discovered by anti-Masons. The anti-Masons had made several attempts to post their propaganda on the CompuServe Masonry Forum itself, but they were quickly booted off. They were, however, able to find a home on several of the CompuServe religious forums, and the campaign of lies began. Of course, along with that was nearly non-stop reference to where so-called "true Christians" could buy "proof" of the anti-Masonic charges and support "God's" work. This was indeed a cleverly disguised moneymaking scheme that was successful for a number of years.

I personally learned how wrong I was about the work of Brothers de Hoyos and Morris when I began taking part in what would become known as the "CompuServe Anti-Masonic Debates." These were a series of debates, *or nasty arguments*, taking place mainly on the various CompuServe religion forums. The anti-Masons would make charges, and knowledgeable Masons would refute the charges. The anti-Masons would then pivot to create new charges, only to then go back to their initial charge *as if it had never been answered*. It was all tactics and games.

These so-called anti-Masons were clever salesmen who were skilled in the bait-and-switch technique. Masons participating in the defense of Freemasonry faced extraordinarily difficult and frustrating times, as they were repeatedly asked the same question. When they answered a question, the anti-Masons would switch the discussion to something else, only to later come back with the original question as if it had never been answered. It was all games. What became clear very quickly was that there was no changing the minds of the ones making the charges. They were fixed in their opinion, and nothing would change it. After all, they were selling anti-Masonic propaganda and making good money doing it! Why would they stop?

The ones who could be changed and influenced by the truth were often the silent readers who had little to no knowledge of Freemasonry. Many of those who had only read the various posts and never stepped out of the shadows had no idea what was true or not. They had no preconceived notions about Freemasonry and initially had no reason to doubt either the anti-Masons or the Masons. These individuals were Christian, and because of the nature of the charges made by the anti-Masons, they were interested in the claims and did purchase material from them because of the subject matter.

Because of the work of the Masonic researchers who took part in these debates, many honest and objective Christians came to see the lies being peddled by these anti-Masonic businessmen. I realized that if Masons ignored these anti-Masonic charges, it would harm the Masonic organization itself due to the persuasive nature of the anti-Masonic sales techniques.

But what is the real difference between a religious fanatic and a religious businessman intent on selling a religious belief? While there may be psychological or philosophical differences between the mindsets, the reality is that neither has a desire to allow *facts* to change their position. You cannot change the mind of someone who *wants* to believe something. It is only when someone is open to the truth that facts have any importance.

While the anti-Masonic frenzy of the 90's has generally passed, a number of these anti-Masonic businessmen still exist and continue to con many individuals.

There is a third form of anti-Masonry that needs to be mentioned. This form of activity is more closely tied to the anti-Masonic businessmen than the fanatic anti-Masons, as making money is their primary goal. This form of anti-Masonry involves businessmen establishing, what appears to be, a Masonic Grand Lodge with the goal of creating Masons. Of course, these bodies are created with no authority whatsoever and are the textbook definition of irregular, but they go a step further. The primary objective of most of these types of self-created grand lodges is to generate profits for the few at the top, while providing little in terms of Masonic benefits to the members.

Prince Hall Masonry uses a term that is very appropriate for these types of Masonic *businesses*. Their term is "bogus Masonry." The term "bogus Masonry" aptly describes these self-created bodies, which resemble moneymaking schemes. I've long felt that there is a need for a third branch in the Masonic tree. What I see as the three branches are: regular Masonry, irregular Masonry, and bogus Masonry. Regular Freemasonry is simply legitimate Freemasonry. It is the Masonry that conducts itself as regular. Irregular Masonry is Masonry that has a problem with its organization or ritual. It is not viewed by regular Freemasonry as regular. However, bogus Masonry differs from irregular Masonry in that many irregular Masonic bodies attempt to practice regular Freemasonry. The problem with irregular Masonry is that it often lacks legitimate origins. Bogus Masonry is usually simply a moneymaking scheme by con men who attempt to personally profit from Freemasonry's reputation.

Some years back, I came across a classic example of bogus Masonry, and it's worth retelling to highlight the danger to regular Freemasonry. In this case, several con men decided to create their own Grand Lodge in an African-American community. They paid close attention to what was going on in the community. They learned of a man who had recently been diagnosed with terminal cancer. He was given only a few months to live. This was a hard-working man with a family. The news of his illness was tough on him, not only because of the fact of the illness, but because he was not a wealthy man and did not know how his family would survive without him.

One evening, a knock came on the door. Several men had come calling, identifying themselves as "the Masons." They told the man and his wife that they had learned of his unfortunate illness and situation. They said that they may be able to help. They said that if this man joined the Freemasons, they would make sure that he would have a Masonic funeral and burial *at no expense* to the family. They said that they would also provide several bags of groceries to the man's widow each week and see to it that his children would remain in school until they graduated or were of age. They said that the fee to join the Masons was $200. They left the man and his wife to consider the offer and said they would return in a few days.

The man and his wife had heard of Freemasonry and knew it to be an honorable organization. But $200 was about all they had in savings. Realizing that this money would not even cover the funeral costs, they felt that joining would be a wise investment for the family's future. They decided that it would be best for him to join. The men returned a few days later, were given the $200, and the sick man was given a dues card and told that he was now a member of the Freemasons.

They left. Nothing more was heard from them.

The man passed away, and, of course, these con men were nowhere to be found. Months after the man passed away, his widow saw one of the men on the street. She approached him in anger and desperation. She wanted to know why they had not come back. She said her husband passed away, and they did *nothing at all*. She reminded him of all that they had promised before her husband's joining.

The man said that there must be a misunderstanding. He said that they fulfill everything as promised. He said that her husband gave them $200 and that this was the "Master Mason's Package." He said that they said a prayer in the lodge for the man and recorded his name in their list of "honored members." He said that what she was talking about was the "33rd Degree Package." He said that this package would have cost $5,000. Of course, the woman realized that she had been tricked by this thief.

While she realized this man's nature, she did not know that he was only *pretending* to be a Mason. From that day on, *anyone* who identified himself as a Freemason was viewed by her and everyone she could tell as a thief and a con man. This group of bogus Masons, thieves, and con men not only deeply damaged and hurt this family but also the whole of Freemasonry with their deception.

This is why I believe that special notice should be taken of this particular brand of anti-Masonry. The damage it does to individuals, the community, and Freemasonry itself cannot be minimized. It must be exposed and by every legal measure crushed out.

No matter what we like, dislike, want, or reject, anti-Masonry has been a thorn in the side of Freemasonry for nearly as long as it has existed. The limitations of this paper do not allow for all accounts of anti-Masonry around the world. Religious fanatics and con men have *not* been the only anti-Masons. Political dictators, as well as anyone seeking to destroy freedom, have been strongly opposed to Freemasonry. Even a few world and religious leaders, such as Pope Leo 13th and US President John Adams, have been famous anti-Masons. Albert Pike has long been a target of anti-Masons due to his difficult-to-understand or open-to-interpretation language. But it is not just Pike's language that has been a point of confusion or attack. Many Masonic words and phrases are simply archaic and odd-sounding to the ear. They are ripe for exploitation by those seeking to profit from misunderstanding.

The early 1900s were a time of more than a few notable Masonic con men, including Matthew McBlain Thomson and his notorious American Masonic Federation, and the almost comical "TK and his Great Work," whose real name was John E. Richardson.

Anti-Masons have also been capable of serious damage to Freemasonry. Space does not permit a close examination of the

William Morgan Affair. Still, the effects of this anti-Masonic attack nearly destroyed the whole of Masonry in the New England states and even more areas of the US in the 1820s, and for a good 20 or so years later.

But, with all that anti-Masonry has done, or tried to do, Freemasonry still exists. We are stronger because of the trials and tribulations of these attacks. I imagine that if anti-Masonry did not exist, Freemasonry could become complacent and disconnected from its goals and philosophy. So, we must learn to live with the dark to enjoy the light.

Notes

1. Tatsch, J. Hugo. "The Rise and Development of Anti-Masonry in America 1737- 1826." *Masonic Enlightenment: The Philosophy, History and Wisdom of Freemasonry.* Ed. Michael R. Poll. New Orleans, LA: Cornerstone Book Publishers, 2006. pp 126-138.

2. de Hoyos, Arturo and Morris, S. Brent. *Is it True What They Say About Freemasonry?* Silver Spring, Md. M.S.A., 1994.

Who Attends Business Meetings?

Significant changes in procedure have been witnessed in US Grand Lodges over the past few years. These changes, particularly in how the lodges conduct their business, are of significant importance. Before delving into the specifics of these changes, it's worth noting the intriguing process through which Grand Lodges navigate alterations in their nature, policy, procedures, and laws.

Let's look at a pencil. It's really a handy and ingenious communication tool. On one end, you have a sharp point. The inside writing material was originally made of lead, but today it's graphite. With this end, you can write down whatever you want. It doesn't matter if you're going to do a bit of calculus, an essay, or a love note — whatever you want to write, you can do so with the pencil. On the other end of the pencil is an eraser. Use this end, and you can eliminate anything you have written in error simply by rubbing it a bit. Now, Grand Lodges operate with a similar adaptability. They can make whatever decision they want. They can write whatever laws they want and govern themselves however they see fit. However, if they realize later that something they have done isn't working for them or serving their expectations, they can go back and erase it. They can revert to the status quo before the law change, or they can take a completely different approach. This adaptability is a testament to the flexibility of the Masonic system, reassuring us that changes are not only possible but also manageable.

Now, for longer than any Mason has been alive, lodges in the United States have conducted their business in the Master Mason degree. But over the last ten or twelve years, a number of jurisdictions in the United States decided that they wanted to change this practice. They wanted to give their lodges the option of doing business on the Entered Apprentice, Fellowcraft, or Master Mason degree. Most of the jurisdictions that made this change felt that the degree in which the lodge conducted its business should be left up to the Worshipful Master of the lodge. Today, about half of the jurisdictions in the United States have made this change. The result is that there has been a bit of discussion about this practice, its value, and whether the rest of the jurisdictions should follow suit. Let's look at some of the history of how lodges have conducted their business.

To start with, lodges have not always conducted their business on the Master Mason degree. That was an innovation in the mid-1800s and something that is not done widely outside of the United States. The seeds of this innovation were planted around 1840. In 1843, a convention of Grand Lodge officers from the US was held in Baltimore, Maryland. This is commonly known as the Baltimore Convention, but actually, there were a number of such conventions that were held between 1843 and 1847. During this time, numerous details were hammered out regarding the desired norms for Masonic jurisdictions in the United States. There was also a rekindling of the effort to have one Grand Lodge for the entire United States, but this was wisely voted down. A number of useful decisions came out of this time, one being the introduction of dues cards. It was felt that it would be beneficial for Masons to have dues cards to prove their current membership. Today, I doubt any US jurisdiction would seriously consider giving up the practice of issuing dues cards. But some of the decisions turned out to be a bit of a hard sell. One initially unpopular decision was the concept that the business of a lodge should be the concern only of Master Masons. It was felt that a lodge of Master Masons should be the only degree in which the business of the lodge should be discussed. Entered Apprentice and Fellowcraft Masons should no longer be present when the business of the lodge was discussed.

I find the decision to transition from the Entered Apprentice degree to the Master Mason degree to be an interesting one, given the assumptions that were made and remain valid in many areas to this day. I'd like to examine some of these assumptions, as well as how lodges operated prior to the 1840s.

Since I am most familiar with Louisiana Masonry, I'd like to look at the situation through the eyes of Louisiana Freemasonry. To start with, Louisiana was not part of the Baltimore convention. The Grand Lodge of Louisiana did not send representatives to any of the conventions. From what can be understood from the few early records that we have, it seems that Louisiana Masonry operated much like French Freemasonry. Some lodges worked in various languages as well as various Masonic rituals. This was just how we had always operated.

Lodges in Louisiana normally opened and conducted their business on the Entered Apprentice degree. When the Fellowcraft or Master Mason degrees were going to be conferred, they had the option of opening in whatever degree they chose. Much was left to the discretion of the Worshipful Master. However, when we say that the lodges conducted their business on the Entered Apprentice degree today, it creates misunderstandings about the role of the Entered Apprentice or Fellowcraft Masons in these lodges.

One of the key points that needs to be understood about early Louisiana Masonry is that so much of its early operation was based on the practices of French Freemasonry. This French practice would include a defined role for the Entered Apprentice and Fellowcraft Masons in the lodge. In short, their job was to learn

Freemasonry. Period. They were expected to learn all aspects of Freemasonry so that when they became a Master Mason, they would be fully qualified to participate with the other Masons intelligently. So, the lodges in France, as well as in Louisiana, would not only *allow* the Entered Apprentices and Fellowcrafts to come into the lodge, but they would *expect* them to come in. They would sit in reserved areas and observe the operation of the lodge. They did not speak or participate in any of the activities of the lodge. They did not have the privilege of questioning anything, speaking in lodge (unless they were answering a direct question from a Master Mason), voting, nor holding any office. Their sole task in the lodge was to observe and learn as much as possible about the lodge operation. They would quietly sit and watch the Master Masons conduct business.

Entered Apprentice and Fellowcraft Masons would often be assigned certain tasks or projects that would typically involve learning various aspects of the Masonic philosophy or symbolism. They would deliver lectures on what they learned with the Master Masons prepared to challenge their understanding and ensure they grasped the material. While I have been addressing early French and Louisiana Masonry, this practice was certainly not limited to them alone. Almost all Freemasonry around the world operated in much the same manner. It was in this environment of learning and teaching that early Masonry existed.

Following the Baltimore Convention, Freemasonry in most areas of the United States became far more standard in practice. One area that became standard was the change in how business was conducted in the lodge. Louisiana, not being part of the conventions, was a bit late with making this switch, and it was not until following 1850 that the Grand Lodge of Louisiana switched to conducting business on the Master Mason degree. After this time, I know of no "US jurisdiction that conducted business in any degree other than Master Mason. In earlier times, Freemasonry did not just initiate candidates into membership. Freemasonry taught its members specific practices proven over time. Having Entered Apprentice Masons present during a business meeting was an excellent educational tool. So, what was the motivation to change to the Master Mason degree?

The desire for all of Masonry in the United States to be near copies of each other has been matched by its desire to be unique in the world of Freemasonry. We wanted to all be alike within the United States but different in many aspects from Masonry outside of the US. We did not wish for lodges in any US jurisdiction to work in different rituals or different languages. We were also not afraid to innovate beyond the norm of Masonic practice outside the US if we felt it was in our best interest. It seems that the switch from doing business on the Entered Apprentice degree to the Master Mason degree was one of those changes that simply wanted to be done.

I've heard interesting, but unproven theories as to why US Masonry made the switch to conducting business on the Master Mason degree. It was stated that because Freemasonry was hit so very hard during the so-called "Morgan Affair," the lodges that survived, or were established after the events, wanted safeguards in place to lessen the chances of a repeat series of events. The feeling seems to have been that one who joined Masonry could not fully be trusted until he was a Master Mason. It seems the feeling could have been that the business of the lodge was not for the ears or eyes of anyone but a Master Mason. It doesn't matter if this theory played a major part, contributed in some way, or had no impact; I find it an interesting theory. The fact is that the US Masonic community did make the decision to switch from business on the Entered Apprentice to business on the Master Mason degree. *Something* must have motivated them to do so.

Now, let's fast forward about 100 years to right after WWII. The war was over; there was peace for a time, and things looked very promising for the United States. There was a swell in Masonic membership. The Grand Lodges accommodated the many new members by expanding the infrastructure of the various jurisdictions. I see this rapid growth as the birth of the "club mentality" in US Freemasonry. But the increase in new members was not to last. By the 1970s, Grand Lodges saw a slowing and then a diminishing of new members. They became worried about the large machines that had been created to manage all the new members. It was not a good time for US Masonry.

Freemasonry in the US struggled for some years until a string of bestselling books and movies came out starting in the 1980s & 90s with Freemasonry as the subject. They portrayed Freemasonry in a positive, if mysterious, light. All of a sudden, petitions started coming into the lodges. Were the hard times over? Did we turn the corner and begin moving in the right direction? Maybe, but maybe not.

While the number of petitions showed a dramatic upswing, the number of demits and suspensions for non-payment of dues over the following years was also noteworthy. Yes, many joined, but they soon left. Why?

The books and movies portrayed Freemasonry as a group of enlightened mystics with something akin to the secrets of life as the reward for joining. And what was found in too many lodges? A group of old men reading minutes and arguing over bills. There was absolutely nothing mystical or esoteric in the meetings. No enlightenment, no education, no inspiring members teaching life lessons — nothing but donuts and coffee. Not only were the meetings far from enlightening, but they were also far from interesting. It was not a matter of the lodge experience failing to be *everything* that they expected; it was *nothing* like what they expected. So, they left.

But not everyone left. A small group of young Masons did remain. They clearly saw the lacking in the lodges. They work towards (and hope upon hope to see) a change in operation. The problem is that the lack of anything significant has become the accepted lodge experience. Too many older Members do not want education, or symbolic study, or anything but the way things are in the lodge. Short of a revolution or waiting for funerals, what can the young ones do?

Because many lodges are suffering from a lack of qualified members going through the chairs, new Masons joining are snapped up for lodge office if they show the slightest bit of potential. It is here that the new members can benefit from the traditional methods of Masonry.

If the young, new Masons have the opportunity to observe the operation of the lodge, they will have approximately six to eight months (average) between their Entered Apprentice initiation and their Master Mason degree to gain a basic understanding of lodge operations. They will be far more experienced than a brand-new Master Mason with no idea of how to operate a lodge, being thrown into the office right after their degree. It's very true that if nothing else changes, many of these might drop out before receiving their Master Mason degree. Of course, the lack in too many lodges will also be realized, and some will find it unworthy of their time, but not all. The ones who remain will be more experienced.

Look, unless you have your head buried in the sand, we all know that there is something seriously wrong in too many lodges. It's not too late to turn things around, but we need to act now. We are an Order that provides moral education to its members by symbolic instruction following initiations. We are special. We are not a club for old men seeking to feed their egos or gather with friends a couple of times a month for social visits. We have a responsibility to who and what we claim to be. We can either do what is right or be a part of the problem.

Business meetings with Entered Apprentices and Fellowcrafts should never be to give a voice or vote to those who are not Master Masons. A vote in the lodge, as well as its leadership, is for experienced Master Masons. The role of Entered Apprentices and Fellowcrafts is to sit quietly and learn. Period. It is the duty of Master Masons to teach the less informed. Every meeting of the lodge is an opportunity for education. Just like physical exercise, the more we do it, the better our Masonic health. Step by step, we can improve.

What each Grand Lodge does is ultimately up to them. We can take whatever direction we wish to take, or we can flounder with inaction. The choice is always ours. My hope is that we choose education and do all we can, by every means possible, to make sure we educate our members and give them every chance to be what we should be — educated Freemasons.

THE US MASONIC RITUAL

I n the United States, there is, for the most part, one accepted craft ritual. It is the ritual, or a version of it, that is worked in the vast majority of the lodges. It is the ritual hammered out by Thomas Smith Webb in the late 1700s. It's known, unofficially, as the "Webb Ritual," the "Preston / Webb Ritual," the "York Rite," and even "the American Rite." But in most cases, it is simply known in the U.S. as "the craft ritual." It is most often called by no name because a name is not really necessary.

To better understand the situation, consider a small town with only one grocery store. The grocery will undoubtedly have a name. It may be named *The Central Grocery*, or *Joe's Grocery*, or whatever name they gave it. But the point is that because there is only one grocery in that town, they can just call it "the grocery." "I'm going to the grocery." Anyone told this in that town would know exactly the store being talked about. Sure, if there were more than one grocery store, they would have to identify which one, like, "I'm going to *Joe's Grocery*."

This is the same situation that exists in most areas of US Masonry. When we, in the US, talk of the craft lodge, we are almost always talking about one ritual and one rite.

Sure, by now, many have heard about those ten Scottish Rite craft lodges under the jurisdiction of the Grand Lodge of Louisiana. But it's a big country, and almost everywhere else there is just one ritual.

In his paper, "The Webb Ritual in the United States,"[1] Silas Shepherd tells us of the Masons involved in the development of what would become the ritual used by most of Masonry in the United States.

It would seem that just following the American War of Independence, Freemasonry in the United States went through something of an identity crisis. The lodges and provincial Grand Lodges in the new country were cut off from their mother bodies, mainly in the United Kingdom. There was a period when the future of Masonry in the youthful United States of America was uncertain.

Some felt that maybe there should be one Grand Lodge for the entire country. Suggestions were made that perhaps even George Washington should become the first Grand Master. Others felt that if the states were to be truly important pieces in a whole, and that the country was based on the collective authority of the states, then maybe each state should have a sovereign and independent Grand Lodge.

When the debates were over, the new country settled on the concept of one Grand Lodge per state, but they also agreed, in theory, on one ritual per state, including the suggestion that they should be one language, which would be English. The idea for Masonry in the United States seemed to be that every state was desired to be independent, yet modeled after the others. It would seem that being like others was good, and being unlike everyone else was not good. Over time, this concept did create problems.

One problem was that everyone was not alike. Just to give one example, in 1803, the young United States grew in size by almost a third when it obtained from France the massive section of land known as the Louisiana Purchase. At the heart of this purchase was the very important port of New Orleans. But this was a French territory with most of the citizens speaking French and proud to be of French heritage.

Masonry, as best as we can tell, had existed in New Orleans since 1752. Its nature and language matched its members, meaning French. Upon arriving in the area, English-speaking American Masons found that the Masonry in New Orleans differed significantly from that in the rest of the US. This discrepancy became a problem for them and led to Masonic conflict for many years to follow. But since we know that more than one Masonic ritual exists in the world, does it help, hurt, or not matter at all if we limit our lodges to only one ritual? In my opinion, and from the standpoint of initiation, it doesn't matter at all. The differences in rituals are all a matter of choice, a matter of preference, or even just what is available in the area. At best, it's all a matter of taste.

Despite the variations in words, actions, and overall feel, all Masonic rituals share a common core—the Hiramic Legend. It is this legend and the symbolic teachings it embodies that distinguish a Masonic initiation from other forms of initiation.

The validity of an initiation in Masonic practice is not determined by the specific ritual used, but by its profound impact on the candidate. Any of the Masonic rites have the potential to resonate deeply with the candidate, or not. The real challenge for lodges lies not in practicing different rituals, but in ensuring that their initiations are indeed valid, resonating deeply with the candidates.

But in reality, even with the claims of many that there is one craft ritual in the United States, over time, these rituals have changed from jurisdiction to jurisdiction. This adaptability of Masonic rituals, where some variations are minor and others are large, fosters a sense of flexibility and open-mindedness. It is far more likely that Masonic craft rituals are identical to each other within a jurisdiction than from jurisdiction to jurisdiction. It is because jurisdictions are sovereign and independent that they have made changes to their own rituals independently, and over time. These changes are often unique to their jurisdiction.

The 1700s and early 1800s were very creative times in Freemasonry. During the time when the Webb Ritual would become the ritual for the bulk of U.S. Masonry, there were many beautiful systems of Freemasonry created around the world. In many areas, multiple rituals worked side-by-side, reflecting the rich nature of Masonic initiation. The enlightened do not view one ritual as better or superior to another, but only as a different path to reach the same destination.

The fact that Masonry in the United States does not utilize all of the different rituals can be viewed as a missed opportunity for variety in lodge meetings. Still, really, in itself, that is only a minor inconvenience.

On the other hand, there is a misunderstanding, or a lack of understanding, concerning the nature of the Masonic Rites. This misunderstanding may exist because of the way that Freemasonry developed in the United States.

The two Masonic Rites that are dominant in the United States are the York Rite and the Scottish Rite. The Scottish Rite, or more correctly, the Ancient and Accepted Scottish Rite, is a 33-degree Masonic system. It was created in 1801 in Charleston, South Carolina. The rituals used by this Rite come from older systems and rituals, mainly from France. The other major Masonic rite in the U.S. is commonly known as the "York Rite" and concludes with the degree of Knight Templar. Sometimes also known as the "American Rite," it was hammered out around the same time that Webb was working on his craft rituals.

Albert Mackey used the term "American Rite" rather than "York Rite" as he felt the system was distinctly an American creation, and to avoid confusion with systems and degrees of like name in England. Mackey was not successful in changing the official name of the rite, and "York Rite" has become the popular and accepted name.

Because of the popularity of the two high-degree Masonic systems that have survived in the U.S., and the desire for there to be only one craft ritual, a possibly unforeseen problem has developed. The problem, when viewed from a Masonic ritualistic standpoint, is that for something to be a Masonic Rite, it must begin in the craft lodge and then conclude at whatever final degree exists for that rite. The first degree of any Masonic rite must be the Entered Apprentice Degree.

The situation for the United States, on first notice, is that we have two high-grade Masonic rites that appear to begin *after* the Master Mason degree and then continue to the completion of the system. Most Masons in the United States pay little attention to the degree progression and simply accept that the Masonic rites, the high-grade bodies, begin *after* the craft lodge degrees. They appear separate and independent from craft lodge Masonry.

Let's look at this situation. A good illustration for this discussion is an old Masonic print titled "The Steps of Freemasonry." I find this piece of art very interesting. What I like about this particular piece of artwork is not that it portrays the actual nature of the Scottish Rite and the York Rite, but that it portrays how Freemasonry is worked from purely an organizational standpoint in the United States. I'd like to take a moment to examine this art and see exactly what it is telling us as to how we view the Masonic rites.

The artwork is created in the shape of a pyramid, with a base and two sets of steps leading up each side. If you look on the side labeled the Scottish Rite, it shows a step for each of the degrees and finally the degree of Sovereign Grand Inspector General, which is the 33rd and last degree. On the York Rite side, it also shows steps along with figures representing each of the degrees of the York Rite, concluding with its final step, the degree of Knight Templar. Also, if you look in the center area of the pyramid, there is an arch, and inside the arch, there are a number of little figures which represent different organizations. This grouping of figures is identified as *Allied Organizations*. This collection is composed of organizations such as the Shrine, Grotto, the Eastern Star, and

The Steps of Freemasonry

other Allied Organizations. These organizations are outside of the craft lodge or outside of the actual rites of Freemasonry.

At the base of the pyramid, the craft lodge is depicted as the foundation, symbolizing its role as the starting point for all Masons. The three steps represent the degrees of Entered Apprentice, Fellowcraft, and Master Mason. Figures ascending these steps can be seen, suggesting the path to the Scottish Rite or the York Rite. The artwork conveys the idea of three distinct paths: the Craft Lodge steps, the steps of the Scottish Rite, and the steps of the York Rite.

The Allied Organizations, depicted higher up the steps, are separate from the craft lodge and the rites of Freemasonry. The Shrine, positioned higher on these steps, historically required a Scottish Rite 32nd degree or a Knight Templar in the York Rite for membership. However, this prerequisite has since changed, and one now only needs to have received the third degree to become a Shriner.

Now, if you take the Allied Organizations out of consideration and away from the image, you are left with the steps for the Scottish Rite, the York Rite, and the craft lodge degrees. The art appears to suggest that you have three separate entities. Since the craft lodge serves as the foundation piece, once you have completed the steps of the craft lodge, you can then advance to the steps of the Scottish Rite or York Rite. The fact is that the Scottish Rite and the York Rite are both complete systems of Masonry with their own unique craft lodges. A *system of Masonry* is another way of saying, *Masonic rite*. This artwork creates a misunderstanding as to the nature of a Masonic rite. Both the York Rite and the Scottish Rite begin their degree structure, or steps, in the Entered Apprentice degree. What is *not* delivered in this piece of art is that both the Scottish Rite and the York Rite have their own unique craft lodge rituals. All that is represented is *the* craft lodge. So, you don't realize that instead of two sets of steps with a common foundation in the craft lodge, it should be two complete sets of steps, each with its own individual craft lodge steps. Neither the Scottish Rite nor the York Rite begins its degrees *after* the Master Mason degree. The Scottish Rite and York Rite begin their systems in their own unique craft rituals.

In the New Orleans area, there are ten lodges under the jurisdiction of the Grand Lodge of Louisiana, which work in the Ancient and Accepted Scottish Rite craft lodge ritual. This is the actual first three degrees of the Scottish Rite, also known as the Scottish Rite blue lodge degrees.

As a side note, the Scottish Rite craft lodges in the New Orleans area have never been known by the term "Red Lodge." The term "Red Lodge" began and has been used in various places around the world to refer to Scottish Rite craft lodges, but not in New Orleans.

Regardless of how the poster "The Steps of Freemasonry" illustrates the nature of Freemasonry, the York Rite and the Scottish Rite each have their own unique foundational or craft lodge ritual. The foundational or craft lodge ritual for the York Rite is the ritual used in most craft lodges in the United States. The foundational or craft lodge ritual for the Scottish Rite is limited, with rare exception, to the rituals used by the ten lodges under the jurisdiction of the Grand Lodge of Louisiana. These ten lodges comprise the 16th Masonic District of the Grand Lodge of Louisiana. In other areas of the world, however, the Scottish Rite craft ritual is one of the most popular of craft lodge rituals.

Understanding the easily misunderstood nature of the American Masonic rites requires a look at the very early days of Masonry in the United States. The early desire of the Masons in the new United States of America for each state to have a single Grand Lodge and ritual led to a situation where it was impossible to have multiple rituals approved in any jurisdiction. This historical context is crucial to understanding the structure and evolution of Freemasonry in the US.

When the 33-degree Ancient and Accepted Scottish Rite was created in 1801 in Charleston, South Carolina, a difficult situation already existed in that state. Without delving into the complex history of Masonry in England, there were two Grand Lodges in South Carolina that traced their roots to English Masonry, but with different styles.

For a deeper understanding of the early history of English Freemasonry, it's recommended to study the philosophies of the Ancients and the Moderns. These two Masonic philosophies resulted in two competing Grand Lodges in England, one commonly known as the Moderns and the other the Ancients. In 1813, they overcame their differences and joined together to create the United Grand Lodge of England.

In South Carolina in 1801, each of these English-style Grand Lodges existed in the state. This presented problems to the rest of the US Grand Lodges because of their desire to have only one Grand Lodge per state. On the surface, both of these Grand Lodges in South Carolina seemed perfectly regular, but the desire of the balance of US Grand Lodges was for these two bodies to merge into one. The problem was that the members of these two Grand Lodges had a strong dislike of each other. They did not want to merge as each believed their own Grand Lodge possessed the correct Masonic philosophy.

The problems created by these two Grand Lodges, along with their resistance to merging, created an impossible situation for the Ancient and Accepted Scottish Rite when it was established in Charleston in 1801.

Simply put, the idea of a third body, the supreme council, controlling craft lodges in that state, was unthinkable. The two Grand Lodges in South Carolina eventually put aside their differences, merged, and became the Grand Lodge of South Carolina.

The Scottish Rite apparently traded its craft lodges for existence and only worked as an organization from the fourth degree onward. By doing this, the US Masonic community could maintain its desire for one Grand Lodge and one ritual approved in each state.

In Louisiana, while these ten lodges working in the Scottish Rite ritual are under the jurisdiction of the Grand Lodge, the simple fact that more than one ritual existed created great problems in Louisiana Masonry in the mid-1800s.

The desire for one Grand Lodge and one ritual nearly tore Masonry apart in the state. This concept of one Grand Lodge and one ritual per state also created misunderstandings about Masonic rites themselves.

As shown in the poster, the craft lodge became almost a separate entity rather than the foundational degrees of our Masonic rites.

A Masonic ritual is simply the vehicle used to deliver a Masonic initiation. If it were a play, it would be the script. A Masonic Rite is a particular type of ritual, encompassing all the degrees associated with it. Throughout history, there have been many different Masonic rites and rituals. Each of the historic Masonic rituals and rites has its own unique beauty and manner of symbolic instruction.

In the early history of Masonry in the United States, we did have more Masonic rites than we do today. The Order of the Royal Secret, the French or Modern Rite, and the Egyptian Rite of Memphis are just a few of the rites once worked in the United States.

While the creative time in our Masonic history, when new Rites and rituals were commonplace, seems to have passed, who knows what tomorrow will bring? For all I know, a new wave of Masonic rites and rituals could be in our future. If there is one thing of which I'm certain, it is that no matter what we have today, it will at some point change.

Notes

1. Shepherd, Silas. "The Webb Ritual in the United States." *Masonic Enlightenment: The Philosophy, History and Wisdom of Freemasonry.* Ed. Michael R. Poll. New Orleans, LA: Cornerstone Book Publishers, 2006. pp 10-17.

Masonic Rites/Appendant Bodies

W hen I first embarked on my journey in Freemasonry, a wise Past Master shared a profound insight with me, "You are entering a true college, a great college! The education you will gain from Masonry is more valuable than you can fathom." After 50 years of being a Mason, I wholeheartedly echo his sentiment. I am convinced that my learning from Masonry will continue until my last breath. It is an inexhaustible source of profound wisdom, but the responsibility to delve into this wealth of knowledge lies on my shoulders. Each of us shares in this responsibility.

In 1875, Albert Mackey wrote a paper titled *"Reading Masons and Masons Who Do Not Read."* In that paper, he ended it with a most interesting line, "The ultimate success of Masonry depends on the intelligence of her disciples."[1] I find that a fascinating statement, as he seems to qualify the "ultimate success" of Freemasonry as well as the intelligence of its members. Mackey is not telling us that Masonry is successful *because* of the intelligence of its members. He is telling us that Masonry *will be* successful *if* it has intelligent, reading members. Our lodges will have intelligent members if they provide quality Masonic education, and our members take advantage of it. If the lodges offer nothing more than a hot meal and a reading of the minutes, or if the members turn their back on Masonic education when it is offered, then the "ultimate success" that Brother Mackey spoke of will not occur.

The success of a lodge is intricately tied to the level of understanding and mastery of a wide range of Masonic educational subjects available to its members. A thriving lodge doesn't demand every member to be a master of the ritual, but its officers and a significant portion of the lodge will undoubtedly possess such proficiency. It's crucial for us to grasp certain fundamentals for the prosperity of the lodge and our personal growth.

An often overlooked yet significant aspect of Masonic education is the nature of Masonic Rites. In the US, there's a prevalent confusion or limited understanding of the differences between a Masonic Rite and an appendant body. Some even hold firmly to incorrect opinions. It's essential to understand that a Masonic Rite and an appendant body are distinct entities, and this understanding is a vital part of a complete Masonic education plan.

In the US, it is common today to believe that an *appendant body* is anything other than a craft lodge. Too often, I read in US Masonic publications and hear in lectures that the York Rite and the Scottish Rite are *appendant bodies.* Such a belief differs from the original understanding of how Rites were viewed and is different from how they are currently recognized in most areas outside the United States. Regardless, today the York Rite and Scottish Rite are often listed alongside organizations such as the Shriners, Grotto, Eastern Star, etc. When questioned why these two Rites are considered appendant, I'm usually either given a blank stare or told the bodies are "appendant" or "attached to" the craft lodge. I'm told they are organizations a Mason can join after receiving his Master Mason degree. That's a misunderstanding of the nature of a Masonic Rite. Of course, groups such as the Shriners, the Grotto, the Eastern Star, and others *are* appendant bodies. As a prerequisite, many of these organizations require membership in a craft lodge (obtaining the Master Mason degree). And here seems to be the source of a long-held confusion about Masonic Rites.

So, why would I say that the York and Scottish Rites differ from the Shrine, Grotto, etc.? Why do I say that they are *not* appendant bodies? Well, as their names suggest, the York Rite and the Scottish Rite are Masonic *Rites* or systems of Freemasonry. A Rite, or system of Freemasonry, is a collection of unique rituals that begin in the Entered Apprentice degree and conclude in their final degree. As Albert Mackey tells us:

"The original system of Speculative Masonry consisted only of the three Symbolic degrees called, therefore, Ancient Craft Masonry. Such was the condition of Freemasonry at the time of what is called the revival of 1717. Hence, this was the original Rite or approved usage. So it continued in England until the year 1813, when at the union of the two Grand Lodges, the "Holy Royal Arch" was declared to be part of the system; and thus, the English Rite was made legitimately to consist of four degrees.

But on the Continent of Europe, the organization of new systems began at a much earlier period. By the invention of what are known as the high degrees, a multitude of Rites were established. These Rites include the French Rite, the Swedish Rite, and the Rectified Scottish Rite, among others. All of these agreed on one important essential. They were built upon the three Symbolic degrees, which in every instance constituted the fundamental basis upon which they were erected."[2]

The important point is that while a Masonic Rite is a collection of rituals that are similar or related in content, it is not an organization itself. A Masonic Rite is not under the jurisdiction of any

Masonic body or organization. A Masonic body uses or works in the rituals of a Masonic Rite.

A Masonic ritual is the script used to confer degrees, open lodges, and is the words of our catechism. A regular Masonic craft ritual will contain the Hiramic Legend, a central narrative in Freemasonry that symbolizes the journey of the individual Mason. And while the three craft degrees follow a logical storyline, they can sometimes be quite different from other rituals of the same degree. These differences can be looked at as the various *Rites* of Freemasonry. The Scottish Rite and the York Rite are both considered *Rites* because they start with their own unique craft lodge degrees and rituals. You can think of the different Rites as different ways of telling the same story.

Over time, translators and editors adapted rituals to suit the lodges that used them or to address what was deemed important for Masons in specific areas. For instance, a language problem existed when Speculative Freemasonry was taken from England to France in its early days. It was necessary to translate the English craft rituals into French if there was any hope of successfully spreading Freemasonry in France. When this translation was done, some consideration for French culture was given. The French rituals told the same story as the English rituals, but the way the story was told differed slightly in the French versions; this led to the development of the French Rite.

When we compare early English and French rituals, it is easy to see that the French rituals became more theatrical. The French rituals also spent more time on aspects of symbolism than the English. This has much to do with the two cultures, and the differences in the rituals reflect the differences between those two cultures. But what does it mean in practice to have different rituals? In the New Orleans area, you can today see two forms of Masonic craft rituals (two Rites) in practice,[3] both in the English language. One is the York Rite craft ritual (English in nature), and the other is the Scottish Rite craft ritual (French in nature). In a

(9)

LIST OF LODGES IN ACTIVITY

UNDER THE JURISDICTION OF THE GRAND LODGE OF THE STATE OF LOUISIANA

LODGES OF YORK RITE,

Meeting at New Orleans, in Rampart street.

No 1. PERFECT UNION—Founder of the Grand Lodge.—Lucien Hermann, Master; H. B. Cenas, S. W.; Louis Lebeau, J. W.

At New Orleans, in Urselines street.

No. 3. CONCORD—Founder of the Grand Lodge.—J. M. Moreau, Master; F. L. Reinecke, S. W.; P. A. Huard, J. W.

At New Orleans in St. Claude street.

No. 4. PERSEVERANCE—Founder of the Grand Lodge.—Francis Calongne, Master; Jules Durrive, S. W.; Thomas Bell, J. W.

At St. Landry, Opelousas.

No. 19. THE HUMBLE COTTAGE.—C. H. Lewis, Master; Evariste Debaillon, S. W.; B. K. Rogers, J. W.

At St. Francisville, West Feliciana.

No. 31. FELICIANA.—Eugene Remondet, Master; W. B. Clupton, S. W.; J. M. Baker, J. W.

At Alexandria, Louisiana.

No. 37. ALEXANDRIA.—William B. Hyman, Master; Allen Tuck, S. W.; Jackson Farrar, J. W.

At Natchitoches, Louisiana.

No. 38. PHENIX.—P. A. Morse, Master; F. Williams, S. W.; N. ———, J. W.

At New Orleans, corner of Common and Tchoupitoulas streets.

No. 39. POINSETT.—A. S. Douglass, Master; H. M. Summers, S. W.; W. H. Van Reuselear, J. W.

At Napoleonville, Parish of Assumption.

No. 44. DESERT.—Clodius Linosier, Master; J. A. Guerard, S. W.; Charles Monot, J. W.

At Greenwood, Parish of Caddo.

No 45. JACKSON.—Alfred Flournoy, Master; D. J. Hooks, S. W.; A. G. Tuqua, J. W.

2

(10)

At New Orleans, at Perseverance Lodge.

No. 46. GERMANIA.—Gustavus Martei, Master; Liebman Rose, S. W.; Theobald Kœning, J. W.

At East Baton Rouge.

No. 47. ST. JAMES LODGE.—D. F. Reeder, Master; J. L. Lobdell, S. W.; P. Cain, J. W.

At St. Martinsville, Attakapas.

No. 48. L'HOSPITALIERE DU TECHE.—Cornelius Voorhic, Master; J. B. Derbes, S. W.; V. A. Fournet, J. W.

At Shreveport, Parish of Caddo.

No. 49. CADDO.—Joel W. Hardwich, Master; L. P. Crain, S. W.; A. T. Alfred, J. W.

LODGES OF THE SCOTCH RITE,
Accumulating the York and Modern Rites.

At New Orleans, in Love street.

No. 1. POLAR STAR—Founder of the Grand Lodge.—Felix Garcia, Master; R. Brugier, S. W.; James Poupart, J. W.

At New Orleans in Plauché street.

No. 3. LIBERAL.—Adrian Nautré, Master; Henry Train, S. W.; Simon Viot, J. W.

At New Orleans, at Perfect Union Lodge.

No. 4. FRATERNAL LOVE.—J. M. Labarre, Master; J. J. Rico, S. W.; M. F. de la Vega, J. W.

At New Orleans, at Perseverance Lodge.

No. 5. THE FRIENDS OF THE ORDER.—Rafael Sagrera, Master; John Bachino, S. W.; Peter Casanas, J. W.

LODGES OF MODERN RITE,
Accumalating the Scotch and York Rites.

At New Orleans, in Plauché street.

No. 4. MASONIC HEARTH.—Antoine Mondelli, Master; Joseph Barnes, S. W.; E. Bertrand, J. W.

From the 1845 Proceedings of the Grand Lodge of Louisiana. Craft lodges were listed together according to their Masonic Rite.

nutshell, the York Rite craft ritual is the foundation of the rest of the degrees of the system known in the US as the York Rite.[4] The Scottish Rite craft ritual is the foundation of the degrees of the Scottish Rite from the 4th to the 33rd (the rest of that system). In many places outside the US, you can see two or more different craft rituals (different Rites) being worked.

Because the evolution of the Masonic Rites seemed to be a bit haphazard (with new Rites and rituals springing up almost at will), they can vary in the number of degrees and even the subject matter of the degrees above the third. A Mason completing the degrees of one Rite will receive a different Masonic experience than a Mason of another Rite. Yes, there is a relationship between the various Rites, but also clear differences. Masonic bodies working in the various Rites today can be seen as selectively exclusive in membership.

A Master Mason cannot visit Masonic bodies or degrees he has not received. In addition, if one has received all the degrees available in one Rite, he is still not entitled to visit corresponding degrees in bodies of other Rites unless he holds membership there as well. But what about a Master Mason in a Scottish Rite craft lodge in New Orleans (or elsewhere)? Can he visit a York Rite lodge of Master Masons?[5] Mackey again instructs us:

> "Hence arises the law, that whatever may be the constitution and teachings of any Rite as to the higher degrees peculiar to it, the three Symbolic degrees being common to all the Rites, a Master Mason, in any one of the Rites, may visit and labor in a Master's Lodge of every other Rite. It is only after that degree is passed that the exclusiveness of each Rite begins to operate."[6]

Yes, a Master Mason in a Scottish Rite craft lodge may visit, and even join, a York Rite craft lodge in New Orleans or elsewhere (and vice-versa).[7] It is part of the education in New Orleans area craft lodges to witness the differences in the rituals of craft lodges available there and begin their understanding of Masonic Rites. It becomes clear to the New Orleans area Scottish Rite Craft Masons that their ritual is the foundation of the whole Scottish Rite. Those Scottish Rite Craft Masons who go on to join a Scottish Rite valley in the Southern Jurisdiction will see that the "storyline" between their 3rd degree and the 4th degree in a valley is a natural progression of their Scottish Rite ritual. Members of a York Rite craft lodge find the 4th degree of the Scottish Rite as recognizable but not a natural flow in their ritual or storyline of the Hiramic Legend. It is clear to a York Rite craft Mason that they have walked into a different version of the ritual account in their craft lodge.

But why are Scottish Rite craft rituals and lodges, which form the foundation of the Scottish Rite degrees from the 4th to the 33rd, so rare in the United States? This rarity is a key point of interest that we will delve into.

The United States, in the aftermath of the American Revolution, witnessed unique developments in Freemasonry. The rituals used worldwide today can be traced back to early English, French, and other European rituals. However, for the purpose of this study, we will focus on the rituals practiced in the United States today.

Most craft Masonry in the early United States came from England, Ireland, or Scotland. While variations in these rituals existed, they all came from the same source. Freemasons in the young United States began reorganizing Freemasonry to suit their likes. Some thought was given to having one Grand Lodge for the entire country. But the final plan was to mirror the example of the organization of the new nation's government, meaning more consideration for the states. With that, one Grand Lodge per state was their choice.

In the years that followed, Freemasonry in the United States began refining its nature and defining what it wanted from each Grand Lodge. The consensus was that each Grand Lodge should be as near as possible a copy of the other. Each would be sovereign and independent, yet very similar in the craft lodge experience of the other Grand Lodges. Of course, being sovereign meant that each was free and entitled to operate as they chose best. Over the years, the Masonic craft ritual for most jurisdictions in the US has begun to vary, sometimes quite a bit, almost defying the original suggested intention.

There seems to have been an early desire for one Grand Lodge per state, one language per Grand Lodge (English), and one ritual for each Grand Lodge (York Rite, also called American/Webb ritual). When we try to understand why they wanted the early Grand Lodges organized this way, we cannot look to any ancient charges for answers. The only logical explanation for why they wanted the US Grand Lodges to be so similar to each other is because that's what they wanted. Period. Most Masons in the New England states spoke English, so the logical choice was English for the lodges. The decisions on how to model the lodges were based on what was commonly used for them.

So, with this one Grand Lodge, one language, and one ritual desire, the various Grand Lodges began to organize and refine themselves. Representatives of the different Grand Lodges would meet regularly to discuss the progress of Masonry in the US. But there was a problem for them in South Carolina. To understand the situation in South Carolina, we will need to take a quick look at England. Without getting into a lengthy history of Freemasonry in England, two groups with different Masonic philosophies developed in England before 1800. As explained in the last paper, one styled themselves as the *Ancients* and the other as the *Moderns*. These two Grand Lodges in England were disapproving of each other. But they did end up settling their differences and, in 1813, merged into what we have today as the United Grand Lodge of England.[8]

In South Carolina, just before 1800, there were also two Grand Lodges, each representing one of the two styles of English

Freemasonry. Both were considered perfectly regular. But the problem remained that the US Grand Lodges' collective desire was for one Grand Lodge per state. Pressure began to be placed on South Carolina for these two Grand Lodges to merge. The problem was that they didn't like each other, and they found the others' Masonic philosophy and practice unacceptable. They did not want to merge.[9]

In 1801, a new development and a new problem came with the creation of another Masonic body in South Carolina. This body did not trace itself back to the English style of Freemasonry but to the French style. Throughout the Caribbean islands, a French style of Masonry called the Order of the Royal Secret, more commonly known as the Rite of Perfection, had gained some popularity. This was a 25° system of French-style Masonry that was unique and quite different than the English style of Freemasonry. The problem was that it seemed poorly organized and often lacked clear central leadership.

A group of Masons who had reached the highest degree in this French system met in Charleston, South Carolina, to discuss the problems with this system. Their solution was to create a new system in 1801 with a better organization and central government. The result of this new creation is what we have today as the 33-degree Ancient and Accepted Scottish Rite.

Remember, this new 33° French-style system, like the old 25° system, was a complete system (Masonic Rite) that included its own unique craft degrees. When this new 33° system was created in Charleston, its "birth certificate" (public announcement) claimed to begin in the craft lodge degrees. But there was an obvious problem. South Carolina was already under considerable pressure because they had *two* grand bodies controlling craft degrees. The US Grand Lodge community sought to merge these two bodies into one. The idea that a *third* body (also controlling craft lodges) would be allowed in that state is unthinkable. For a brand-

The Names of the Masonic Degrees are as follow, viz.

1st Degree called. Enter'd Apprentice.
2 ——————— Fellow Craft.   } Given in the Symbolic Lodge.
3 ——————— Master Mason.   }
4 ——————— Secret Master.
5 ——————— Perfect Master.
6 ——————— Intimate Secretary.
7 ——————— Provost and Judge.
8 ——————— Intendant of the Building.
9 ——————— Elected Knights of 9.   } Given in the Sublime Grand Lodge.
10 ——————— Illustrious Elected of 15
11 ——————— Sublime Knight Elected.
12 ——————— Grand Master Architect.
13 ——————— Royal Arch.
14 ——————— Perfection.
15 ——————— Knight of the East.   } Given by the Princes of Jerusalem, which is a
16 ——————— Prince of Jerusalem.   } Governing Council.
17 ——————— Knight of the East and West.
18 ——————— Sovereign Prince of Rose Croix de Heroden.
19 ——————— Grand Pontiff.
20 ——————— Grand Master of all Symbolic Lodges.
21 ——————— Patriarch Noachite or Chevalier Prussien.
22 ——————— Prince of Lebanus.
23 ——————— Chief of the Tabernacle.   Given by the Council of
24 ——————— Prince of the Tabernacle.   Grand Inspectors, who
25 ——————— Prince of Mercy.   are Sovereigns of Ma-
26 ——————— Knight of the Brazen Serpent.   sonry.
27 ——————— Commander of the Temple.
28 ——————— Knight of the Sun.
29 ——————— K.—H.
30 31 32. ——— Prince of the Royal Secret, Princes of Masons.
33 ——————— Sovereign Grand Inspectors General. ————— Officers appointed for Life.

Besides those degrees, which are in regular succession, most of the Inspectors are in possession of a number of detached degrees, given in different parts of the world, and which, they generally communicate, free of expence, to those Brethren, who are high enough to understand them. Such as Select Masons of 27 and the Royal Arch, as given under the Constitution of Dublin. Six degrees of Maconnerie D'Adoption, Compagnon Ecossois, Le Maitre Ecossois & Le Grand Maitre Ecossois, &c. &c. making in the agregate 52 degrees.

The Committee respectfully submit to the consideration of the Council, the above report on the principles and establishment of the Sublime degrees in South-Carolina, extracted from the archives of the Society. They cannot however conclude, without expressing their ardent wishes for the prosperity and dignity of the Institutions over which this Supreme Council preside; and they flatter themselves that if any unfavourable impressions have existed among their Brethren of the Blue degrees, from the want of a knowledge of the principles and practices, of Sublime Masonry, it will be done away, and that harmony and affection, will be the happy cement of the universal society of Free and Accepted Masons. That as all aim at the improvement of the general condition of mankind by the practice of virtue, and the exercise of benevolence, so they sincerely wish, that any little differences which may have arisen, in unimportant ceremonies of *Ancient* and *Modern*, may be reconciled, and give way to the original principles of the order, those great bulwarks of society, universal benevolence and brotherly love, and that the extensive fraternity of

Free

PLATE 6

The "Birth Certificate" of the AASR showing the original Scottish Rite degree names and structure. Officially titled, "Circular throughout the two Hemispheres" See: R. Baker Harris and James D. Carter, History of the Supreme Council, 33° (1801-1861) (Washington, D.C.: The Supreme Council, 33° Southern Jurisdiction, USA, 1964) pp. 319-325.

new organization with tons of potential, this was a deal-breaking problem and one that they needed to address.

While the early records of the Charleston Supreme Council (known commonly today as the *Supreme Council, Southern Jurisdiction* — the Mother Supreme Council of the World) do not exist, we can assume that there was a strong outside objection (or expected objection) to a new body in South Carolina controlling craft degrees. If the young Charleston Council had ever attempted to work in the craft degrees of the Scottish Rite, it would undoubtedly have been short-lived. But we have no information one way or the other. All we know from the existing records is that at some point, the Supreme Council officially confined its degrees from the fourth to the 33rd. There seems to have been an adjustment period as they figured out what they would do and how they would operate. It was, after all, a brand-new body and Rite. It seems reasonable that the early Charleston Supreme Council decided to give up its craft lodges in trade for the chance to exist. Without question, if the Charleston Council had insisted on working in or controlling Scottish Rite craft lodges, they would have had a short existence. But outside the United States, the Scottish Rite craft lodge ritual is one of the most popular for well-recognized Grand Lodges in Central America, South America, and Europe.

So, to go back to the beginning of this paper and the current belief among many that the York and Scottish Rites are *appendant bodies*. How did we arrive at that way of thinking? Well, a lack of proper Masonic education and human nature are the leading causes of this misconception and misuse of the term. What do we see if we look at the Scottish Rite in almost all areas of the US? Most experience the Scottish Rite as a 29-degree system. The degrees of the Scottish Rite (from what can be seen by most in the US) span the 4th to the 32nd. Many (more than we may assume) view the 33rd degree as an "honorary degree" or award given to some 32nds. They do not see the 33rd as a "real" degree of the Scottish Rite. They are aware of the Supreme Council, but they view it primarily as an administrative body. The York Rite is seen as a collection of loosely associated, independent bodies given the general term of "York Rite." Most view the "craft lodge" as an independent entity of no particular "Rite"— it is just "the craft lodge." Both the Scottish Rite and the York Rite are viewed as *organizations* that a Master Mason can join if he wishes. For many years, it was *necessary* for one with a desire to join the Shriners to first join either the York Rite or Scottish Rite. The York and Scottish Rites held no deeper meaning or importance than being a stepping-stone.

Of course, in way too many cases, if we wanted to learn about Scottish Rite history, a good portion of what we received was the near endless (and pointless) arguments to try and show why one Mason, Joseph Cerneau, was irregular and his Scottish Rite was not a "real" Scottish Rite (as well as wholly undesirable and worthless). In the end, no matter which side you fell on in the "Cerneau regularity question," it provided *no* help at all in understanding the profoundly beautiful philosophy of the Scottish Rite. If Joseph Cerneau were 100% regular and a saint of a Mason, it would change nothing as to the importance of the Scottish Rite any more than if he were the devil's own child. I am not saying that Scottish Rite history is unimportant, but I believe it needs to be studied after understanding the philosophy.

Scottish Rite craft lodges in the US became somehow (and incorrectly) tied to "Cerneau Masonry" and viewed as "irregular Masonry" simply because that is what some said of them. Young Masons were molded into believing that the Scottish Rite is a 29-degree system and that Scottish Rite craft lodges do not, or should not be allowed to exist. So, these lodges (in the US) were either forgotten by some or unknown to others. In time, these young Masons were the senior Masons, and the unfortunate innovation became accepted as law. It is profoundly misleading, uninformed, and dangerous to view the foundation of such an important and beautiful system as the Ancient and Accepted Scottish Rite as irregular and unworthy of use.

And what of the York Rite? Albert Mackey bluntly states:

"In the United States, it has been the almost universal usage to call the Masonry there practiced the York Rite. But it has no better claim to this designation than it has to be called the Ancient and Accepted Rite, or the French Rite, or the Rite of Schroder. It has no pretensions to the York Rite. Or its first three degrees, the Master's is the mutilated one which took the Masonry of England out of the York Rite, and it has added to these three degrees six others which were never known to the Ancient York Rite, or that which was practiced in England, in the earlier half of the 18th century by the legitimate Grand Lodge. In all my writings for years past, I have ventured to distinguish the Masonry practiced in the United States, consisting of nine degrees, as the "American Rite," a title to which it is clearly and justly titled, as the system is particular to America, and is practiced in no other country."[10]

Masonic scholar and historian, Robert Freke Gould, continues in this line of thought with:

"What is commonly known and described as the American Rite, consists of nine degrees, viz.: 1–3, Entered Apprentice, Fellow Craft, and Master Mason, which are given in Lodges, and under the control of Grand Lodges; 4–7, Mark Master, Past Master, Most Excellent Master, and Royal Arch, which are given in Chapters, and under the control of Grand Chapters; 8, 9, Royal Master, and Select Master, which are given in Councils and under the control of Grand Councils. To these, perhaps, should be added three more degrees, namely, Knight of the Red Cross, Knight Templar, and Knight of Malta, which are given in Commanderies, and under the control of Grand Commanderies."[11]

But what is the current view of the York Rite, and which degrees are considered part of the York Rite? From the website titled "York Rite Freemasonry Official Information."

THE YORK RITE STORY

as narrated by

"YORKIE" RITE

(MM-RAM-RSM-KT)

BRANCHES AND DEGREES OF THE AMERICAN, OR YORK RITE

THE SYMBOLIC (BLUE) LODGE
1. Entered Apprentice
2. Fellowcraft
3. Master Mason

CHAPTER OF ROYAL ARCH MASONS
4. Mark Master
5. Past Master
6. Most Excellent Master
7. Royal Arch Mason

COUNCIL, ROYAL-SELECT MASTERS
8. Royal Master
9. Select Master
10. Super Excellent Master

COMMANDERY OF KNIGHTS TEMPLAR
11. Order of Red Cross
12. Order of Malta
13. Order of the Temple

Published by: Educational Bureau
General Grand Chapter, R.A.M.
Box 489
Danville, KY 40423

Pamphlet published in the 1950s by the "Education Bureau General Grand Chapter, R.A.M" and used until around the 1970s showing the degrees of the "American or York Rite" including the craft lodges degrees. Thanks to Taylor Nauta for the photo.

"The York Rite, or more correctly, the American Rite, is based on the early remnants of Craft Masonry that were practiced in the early 1700's. [...] Thus, unlike the Ancient and Accepted Scottish Rite, which claims to hold the power of conferring the first three degrees of Masonry in addition to those under its jurisdiction, those found in the York Rite have rightfully acknowledged the fact that they are considered appendant to those of Ancient Craft Masonry."[12]

What does this mean? Let's look at it.

At some point, the York Rite seems to have "forgotten" (or disowned) its craft lodges. During the late 1900s, the York Rite seemed to disconnect itself from the craft lodge, with its membership open to Master Masons. With this, the craft lodge, the York Rite, and the Scottish Rite became three separate entities, with both *Rites* somehow becoming "appendant" to the "craft lodge." But, to which Rite did the craft lodge belong? None? Interesting explanations and deflections began to develop. Look again at what is written on this website about how some today view the York Rite and how some compare it with the Scottish Rite,

"... unlike the Ancient and Accepted Scottish Rite, which claims to hold the power of conferring the first three degrees of Masonry in addition to those under its jurisdiction."

What? There are no Masonic *Rites* holding "the power of conferring" any of the degrees of Masonry. Masonic *bodies*, not Rites, hold such power. A Masonic Rite is simply a collection of similar rituals. This is, clearly, the heart of the misunderstandings. It is a twisting up of Masonic *Rites* and Masonic *bodies*. At some point, the term "Rite" became confused with "body," and when speaking of the "Scottish Rite" or "York Rite," it came to be understood to mean certain Masonic bodies or organizations. This is a truly misleading and altogether incorrect understanding of the terms.

A Masonic body is an organization that works (labors) in degrees of a Masonic Rite. A Masonic Rite is a collection of similar rituals that begins with the Entered Apprentice Degree (craft degrees) — nothing more, nothing less. Certain Masonic bodies control certain Masonic degrees. A Scottish Rite Lodge of Perfection does not confer the Master Mason degree of its own Rite any more than a York Rite Chapter confers the York Rite Master Mason degree. A *craft lodge* confers the Master Mason degree regardless of the Rite. But then again, a Scottish Rite Lodge of Perfection does not have the authority on its own to confer the 33rd degree any more than a York Rite Chapter confers the Knight Templar degree. Certain Masonic bodies control and confer certain degrees regardless of the Rites being worked. The craft lodge degrees (of any Rite) are conferred in craft lodges and in no other bodies. In the early days of US Freemasonry, it was agreed that craft lodges would be under the jurisdiction of Grand Lodges. (Why this was agreed upon is a question for another paper.) A Grand Lodge is a Masonic body just like the craft lodges under its jurisdictions. The Grand Lodge's ritual in its opening and closing of the Grand Lodge is part of a Masonic Rite, just like the rituals used by the lodges under its jurisdiction.

At some point (maybe born out of the internet's self-indulgent, dubious *wisdom* of Wikipedia), York Rite Masons developed this idea that the "York Rite" begins *following* the Master Mason degree. The "York Rite" became a collection of "independent bodies" and not a collection of related rituals. In the same manner of misunderstanding, Grand Lodges developed the idea that Scottish Rite craft rituals were completely irregular and should never be allowed to be worked by craft lodges under their jurisdiction. Of course, many who held this opinion were perfectly agreeable to receiving the 33rd degree of the Scottish Rite as it was a coveted honor to which they felt wholly entitled. The irony of accepting part of a Masonic system yet rejecting another part of the same system is astonishing.

To go back to Albert Mackey's comment quoted at the beginning of this paper. It may seem that our intelligence and success will be determined by how much we know — how much we read, study, and learn. We are in a most exciting time. Young men do seem to be coming to our doors once again, but they are coming with more questions. They expect reasonable, accurate answers. They read — and more than just the internet. I believe that the next years will determine our ultimate level of success in Freemasonry.

Notes

1. Albert Mackey, *Reading Masons and Masons Who Do Not Read*. Originally published in *Voice of Masonry*, June 1875.

2. Albert Mackey, *An Encyclopaedia of Freemasonry and its Kindred Sciences: comprising the whole range of arts, sciences, and literature as connected with the institution.* (New Orleans, LA: Cornerstone Book Publishers, 2015 reprint of 1916 edition), p. 626.

3. Today, the Grand Lodge of Louisiana allows two different craft rituals to be used in lodges under its jurisdiction: the York Rite craft ritual and the Ancient and Accepted Scottish Rite craft ritual. In 1833, the Grand Lodge of Louisiana changed its Constitution to allow three different craft rituals: the York Rite craft ritual, the Ancient and Accepted Scottish Rite craft ritual, and the French or Modern Rite craft ritual. In 1850, the Grand Lodge of Louisiana again changed its Constitution to allow only York Rite craft rituals to be worked by its lodges. A period of extreme disarray followed, resulting in the Grand Lodge modifying its Constitution to allow a limited number of lodges to work in the Scottish Rite craft ritual. The French or Modern Rite was not revived under the Grand Lodge of Louisiana.

However, elements of the ritual may have blended into a few of the Scottish Rite craft lodges.

4. Considerable debate exists over the use of "York Rite" to identify any of the rituals or degrees in the US identifying themselves as "York Rite." Albert Mackey led an effort to change the term "York Rite" in the US to "American Rite." His effort was not wholly successful, and today "York Rite" and/or "American Rite" is sometimes used, often leading to confusion with new Masons. Albert Mackey was strongly opposed to using the term "York Rite" for the rituals used in the United States. Others were not so firm against its use. Henry Coil says, "It was quite natural and reasonable that the term, *York Rite*, came by common usage to describe both in Britain and America the Craft agrees with the Royal Arch and later the Knights Templar Degree, together with associated degrees of Mark, Past and Most Excellent Master, the Red Cross and Knight of Malta." Henry Wilson Coil, Allen E. Roberts — Editor, Revised Edition. *Coil's Masonic Encyclopedia* (Richmond, VA: Macoy Publishing & Masonic Supply Co., Inc., 1995) p. 560.

5. This question assumes that Fraternal Relations exist between the bodies. When a Master Mason desires to visit another lodge of Master Masons, and it is outside of his jurisdiction (Grand Lodge), then Fraternal Relations must exist before visitation. Your Grand Secretary can determine if recognition exists between various jurisdictions.

6. Mackey, *An Encyclopaedia of Freemasonry* p. 626.

7. Each jurisdiction's rules and laws of visitation and recognition apply.

8. Mackey, *An Encyclopaedia of Freemasonry* p. 815

9. Ibid., 701. *Coil's Encyclopedia*, p. 626-628. Robert Freke Gould, *A Concise History of Freemasonry*. (New Orleans, LA: Cornerstone Book Publishers, 2020 reprint of 1903 edition), p. 421.

10. Mackey, *An Encyclopaedia of Freemasonry* p. 871.

11. Gould, *A Concise History*. p. 424.

12. See: (https://yorkrite.org/wp/what-is-a-york-rite-mason/) Accessed 09/28/2025.

Operative and Speculative Masonry

I was contacted recently by a young Mason with a question about the early history of Speculative Freemasonry. He said that he had initially believed that modern Speculative Masonry evolved out of the old Operative Freemasons, but then he read something that discounted that idea. He wanted to know my thoughts on the matter.

OK, let's delve into the intriguing world of Masonic history. This will be an opinion paper, a logical exploration of the early days of Speculative Freemasonry. We're faced with many missing or non-existent records, leaving much to the best guess of the historian. The history of Operative Freemasonry is even more enigmatic. Yes, we know some things, but so much is anyone's guess, adding to the mystery and allure of our subject.

When you take these situations and couple them with the very valid demand of "you say or write it, you prove it," then it makes for a very problematic situation. Any quick answer can bring discredit to the one saying it. To understand this situation, we need to understand what Operative Freemasonry means, what Speculative Freemasonry means, and what "evolving from" means. Or, at least, we need to agree on some common understanding.

First, what was a lodge of Operative Freemasons? It can be seen as a workers' union of sorts. Skilled workers in the building trade or guilds could find employment through membership in such lodges. Someone would want something built, and they would contract an Operative lodge to build it. The lodge would provide all the workers needed. All the workers would be required to be able to travel to wherever the work site was located. This is what is understood as a "free-mason." One who was a member of an Operative lodge could not be a bondsman, slave, or indentured servant. They needed to be able to travel wherever the jobs would take them.

Another thing about an Operative lodge of Freemasons is that they did not have only stonemasons as members. The buildings built by these lodges also needed carpenters and workers in metal, glass, and other artisans. It was a workers' union of all those who participated in the construction of a building.

We can also find evidence that Operative Lodges were also training schools where young men who desired to one day join the lodge as full members (and workers on building projects) could learn as apprentices. So, an Operative lodge would be a place to learn and obtain work.

Now, if we look at almost any Masonic history book, we will find an English minor aristocrat and alchemist named Elias Ashmole. He was a significant figure in the history of Freemasonry, known for his interest in the occult and his involvement in the early days of the craft. On October 16th, 1646, he was said to have written in his diary that he joined Warrington Lodge. So, what was Warrington Lodge? What does his joining this lodge mean? And is the diary entry accurate?

From available records, Warrington Lodge was an Operative Lodge of Freemasons. It seems that Ashmole joined an Operative Lodge but had no interest in becoming an Operative Freemason. He had other reasons for becoming a member. The suggestion is that this is early evidence of a Speculative Freemason.

As to whether Ashmole's diary account is accurate, well, I have not seen any lodge record of him — maybe there is one, but all that I have seen are reported entries from his diary. The best that I can do is look at the situation from a logical standpoint. I can examine what I know and don't know and give an opinion based on what I believe is probable.

Let's step back for a moment and look at what was happening around that time. If Warrington Lodge was a lodge of Operative Freemasons, it would have been a place of employment for workers in the building trade. Why would they have an interest in someone joining them who was *not* a skilled craftsman?

If what we know about the history of the great European cathedrals is accurate, then the largest and greatest ones were built between approximately 1000 and 1500 AD. By the time Ashmole is reported to have joined, the building trade seems to have gone into a decline. Operative lodges may have needed help finding work for their craftsmen. But again, why would a lodge of Operative Freemasons have any interest in someone who was *not* a skilled craftsman joining them? How could his joining an Operative lodge be of any benefit to anyone? For that matter, what would it be about a trade guild that would be of any interest to someone like Ashmole?

We need to step outside the known information and standard reports to take another look at the situation from both sides. We also need to realize that we can't look at past events using our knowledge of events today. The truth is that the common lodge experience in the US today is dramatically different than the typical US lodge experience from the early to mid-1800s or even 1900s. We must realize that we are wholly unfamiliar with the lodge experience of an Operative lodge in England in the 1600s or earlier.

If we were somehow transported back in time to the initiation of Elias Ashmole, we would undoubtedly be in a very different world. But, even with the clear understanding that the lodge experience of Ashmole was very different from the lodge experience of Masons today, more is needed to answer the *why* of the question. Why would either the lodge or Ashmole have any interest in his initiation taking place?

Let's look at the lodge first.

If this were a lodge of Operative Freemasons and it had been experiencing a good number of years of declining work, it would likely be in some financial trouble. The lodge would need income to cover both its bills and the wages of its workers. If someone like Ashmole was willing to pay to be "accepted" into the Operative lodge, then why not take his money? If any work came, he would *not* be sent out with the other workers. He was not an actual "Free Mason." He was an "Accepted Mason."

When we look at the situation in this light, it is reasonable for such lodges to create a special category for individuals of good character willing to pay the lodge for something akin to honorary memberships. This type of special category would make sense for the lodge, but it does not explain why individuals like Ashmole would have any interest in such a lodge.

From what we know about Elias Ashmole, he was a very accomplished individual. He was an alchemist, an astrologer, a solicitor (English attorney), a founding Fellow of the Royal Society of London, and a collector of many rare manuscripts. He showed interest in basically all seven liberal arts and sciences.

Ashmole was a most interesting and talented man of metaphysical, spiritual, and scientific thought. So, why would he even entertain the idea of joining such a building guild? Well, maybe because this was not just some collection of hard-working laborers.

The Freemasons had always possessed a unique reputation in all the areas where they visited and worked. Most people spent their lives in the small communities where they lived. They would work until nightfall and then come home. This was their life and was repeated each day until they died. It was a big deal when travelers from out of their area came to town.

By the mere fact of their traveling from area to area, the Freemasons grew in knowledge. They became educated in many subjects by exposure to them in their travels. In the evenings, stories were shared from areas they had never seen (and likely would never see). They developed a mystique.

By the 1500s, the Dark Ages were ending, and what would follow was the Reformation and then the Age of Enlightenment. Individuals like Ashmole were some of the early leading figures in this new desire to learn, explore, and grow as humans. With all the subjects that interested Ashmole, the mystique of the Freemasons and their "secrets" must have called to him.

Ashmole was hungry for knowledge and wanted to learn firsthand the Freemasons' "secrets." He reached an agreement with them and was accepted by a lodge. Interestingly enough, after joining, his diary shows him rarely participating in the lodge. There may be good reasons for his lack of participation.

We must remember that an Operative lodge of Freemasons was *primarily* a workers' union. They existed first and foremost to find work for their members. Ashmole could very likely have found the business meetings of the lodges very dull. But that's only a guess based on the man's reported interests and the fact that after joining, he rarely attended.

If the lodge had been active in the areas that interested Ashmole greatly, he might have attended far more often. Again, these lodges, regardless of their reputations, were primarily workers' unions designed to train and find building jobs for their workers. These workers wanted to put food on their tables and went to the lodges to find work. They had a very different reason for going than Ashmole.

Over the next 100 to 150 years, the building trade declined even further. We also find traces of Speculative Lodges of Freemasons during this period. These would be made up solely of those who did not consider themselves Operative Freemasons or construction workers.

When we step back, it does seem a most interesting time. Operative Masons went to the lodge to find work to put food on the table. The Speculative Masons went to lodge to discuss more esoteric subjects alluded to by the Operatives and maybe expand on them.

For one, the lodge was a practical experience designed to find work; for the other, it was an educational experience designed for personal enlightenment. Given their vastly different goals, it seems odd that they would have been mixing at all.

In 1717, the Grand Lodge of England was created to organize lodges of Speculative Freemasons. Speculative Freemasonry took off and spread all over the world like dry houses on fire. To say that it became popular everywhere it was organized is an understatement.

Operative lodges certainly did not benefit from the worldwide growth of Speculative Freemasonry. It was apples and oranges. The Speculative lodges offered what was widely sought by the common man: education and enlightenment.

But, as time passed and interest continued to grow, members wanted to know more of the history of Speculative Freemasonry. Unfortunately, this is where the problems began. Claims of Freemasonry going back to the days of King Solomon were not uncommon. Glorified, royal histories seem to be desired. These wild claims have damaged serious Masonic research and caused some to doubt the ability of Masonic organizations to conduct objective research into their own history. Too much of what was presented as history was fantasy.

Let's try to bring this all together and take a look. The old Operatives made their living by working in the building trade. Speculative Masons make their living from all jobs under the Sun.

The old Operatives met in lodges to train, learn about, and find jobs in the building trade. Speculative Masons met in lodges to discuss theories, ideas, and lessons designed to improve themselves.

Yes, we can find records of some who joined Operative lodges and did not seek involvement in the building trade. Yes, Operative Freemasonry was declining when Speculative Freemasonry was on the rise. Yes, Speculative Freemasonry was created on the perceived model of Operative Masonry. The working tools, jewels, stations, and ranks were tweaked, used, and assigned various moral lessons.

It is not possible to look at Speculative Freemasonry without considering what we know of Operative Masonry. The two are intertwined by centuries of real, imagined, or borrowed association. Speculative Freemasonry is, at the very least, heavily inspired by the model of the old Operatives. That seems clear. However, I don't personally believe that Operative Freemasonry transformed itself into Speculative Freemasonry.

Individuals inspired by the lore of the old Operatives likely created something based on it, incorporating touches they believed suited their needs and wants. It is possible that some who joined Operative lodges with no intention of working in the trade felt that this gave them certain rights to create their own Masonic lodges, even if they were a bit different from the ones they joined.

Anyway, that's my take on the matter. I don't see that we can prove much more than what is already out there without new information being discovered, which is always possible. Of course, in the end, I don't think it matters. The lessons of Speculative Freemasonry are valid and have stood the test of time.

Speculative Masonry does not have to be thousands of years old to be valid. If Masonry is, at all, declining today, it is not because of the lessons taught by our lodges. The problems may be coming from the *lack* of those lessons being taught.

JOINING A MASONIC LODGE

N ot long ago, a young man turned in his petition to a Masonic lodge. Perhaps a relative of his was a Mason, or he learned about Freemasonry from a popular book or movie. Regardless, he expressed his desire to join.

A few weeks after turning in his petition, he received a phone call from a man who told him that he was a member of an investigation committee working on the petition. The committee's role is to ensure that the petitioner is a good fit for the lodge and to answer any questions he may have. He asked the young man if he and two other lodge members could come to his house to meet with him. They met at the appointed time. It was a good meeting. Questions were asked, and everyone learned a bit more about each other.

The committee told the young man that Freemasonry is not an insurance agency. Masonry does not extend health benefits nor give promises of financial aid. While lodges and individual Freemasons have a long and honorable history of assisting those in need, Freemasonry is not designed to be a charitable organization, such as the Red Cross.

Freemasonry is also not a civic association such as the Jaycees or Lions Club. The primary goal of Freemasonry is to take good men and, through moral instruction, give them the keys by which they can, hopefully, make themselves better, happier, and more useful in their lives.

The young man took in all that he was told. He then asked about the history of Freemasonry. He was told that we don't have a complete or clear understanding of all aspects of our beginnings. We know that we are old. As an organization, we go back to around 1717 with the reported creation of the Grand Lodge of England. But many claim that we can trace ourselves to much earlier times — to the days of the old Operative Freemasons. Many also claim that we can trace our philosophy and manner of symbolic education to an even earlier time. Sadly, we just don't have definitive answers. The young petitioner accepted all that he was told, and the committee left. Both sides were satisfied.

The young man was quietly excited. He knew that what he wanted to join was something ancient and significant. He couldn't explain why, but he felt it in his heart. He had done his homework. He had already read popular books and conducted internet searches of Freemasonry. He knew better than to pay attention to the large amount of flash concerning Freemasonry. He ignored the wild supernatural claims and nonsensical satanic charges. He knew that there was something very special about Freemasonry, its manner of instruction by degrees, and the whole Masonic philosophy. He felt a deep sense of anticipation and eagerness about joining.

In a few weeks, a letter came in the mail telling him that the lodge had voted on his petition. The ballot was clear, and the date of the initiation was set. But there were many questions that he had forgotten to ask. One thing that he was unsure about was how he should dress for the initiation. He thought about calling, but then remembered some of the books he owned. In them, the Masons all wore business suits, and some even wore tuxedoes. The photos were not particularly old, so he thought that he should try to match their dress. He knew this was something special, but he assumed they would have told him if they wanted him to wear a tuxedo. So, he decided to wear his suit.

When he showed up at the lodge, a number of the members were wearing old blue jeans and equally faded and worn polo shirts, as well as some in t-shirts. Others looked like they were wearing soiled work clothes and had come directly to lodge from work. He felt out of place in such a casual atmosphere. One of the men laughed when he saw him and asked if he was going to church or a wedding.

The young man waited downstairs and was finally called up for the initiation. This is a significant moment in a Mason's journey, marking the beginning of his formal introduction to the principles and teachings of Freemasonry. But, he felt slightly uncomfortable as the man who came down for him was laughing and told him, "Now you are in for it!" In for what? What did he mean by that?

He was placed in a little room by a kindly, elderly man who seemed sincerely interested in his well-being. This made him feel better. The degree began.

After the degree ended, the young man had mixed emotions. He knew that what he had experienced was something very important, but why was there so much laughter and talking going on? Why did he hear a considerable amount of yelling out instructions? It was clear that some who spoke did not, at all, know their lines (they were stumbling and fumbling over every few words), and others, from everywhere, were telling the officers what to say (and, loudly).

As he was walking around, he also heard about someone's wife being sick and another's cousin who is building a new garage. What did all that have to do with his degree? But afterwards, everyone was so friendly. He couldn't help but feel a sense of confusion and disappointment. Maybe he expected too much. Perhaps Freemasonry is simply a group of men who gather to enjoy each other's company and occasionally participate in outdated and seemingly meaningless rituals.

In time, the young man's feelings about Masonry changed from those before his joining. These were all nice guys. Every time he went to a meeting, he was greeted with smiles, friendly hand-shakes, and inquiries about his health and well-being. He began to feel a sense of belonging and acceptance within the lodge.

There was a mixture of blue-collar workers and professional men. All seemed genuinely interested in the lodge, but most could not really answer even the most basic questions concerning Freemasonry. It was almost as if Freemasonry and the lodge were two completely different things.

Questions on the ritual or history were always passed to one brother, who they said was the "answer man." They were a nice group of men — friends — but there was nothing *special* in the lodge; special in the way he viewed Masonry before he joined. This was a club made up of good guys who would meet a couple of times a month to enjoy themselves. They would visit and share a few laughs during a friendly evening. That seemed to be all that he could expect from the lodge experience. The books clearly were speaking of something else. But what? Who were the Freemasons that he had read about? Did they ever exist? Was it all made up to sell books?

After a few months, the young man found that a TV show was scheduled at the same time as his lodge meeting. It was a show he had been wanting to watch for some time. He chose the show over the lodge. Over the next few months and years, it became increasingly easy to choose many events over the lodge meetings.

Eventually, the young man attended lodge, maybe once or twice a year. He made an effort to attend some of the important meetings. He did so out of a feeling of obligation, not really enjoyment. But he did see some who truly seemed to enjoy each and every meeting. These were the men who kept the lodge alive.

At a few meetings, some of the regular attendees gently scolded him for not attending more of the lodge functions. "You know, the lodge depends on its members, and if you don't support the lodge, it will fail." But what was he to do? Was he truly obligated to visit a place that offered him no benefits beyond a few laughs and a meal? He had tried, but after many months of only hearing a reading of the last meeting, bills that needed to be paid, who was sick, and discussion of the next planned social event, he grew disinterested. He knew that he could spend his time in more productive ways.

So, was he to be blamed, as it was suggested? He even read such things from "ranking" Masons who seemed to put all responsibility for the success or failure of a body on his simply attending, regardless of what was offered. The man at the top was never to blame, and even if he was, nothing was ever done. There was no accountability for poor leadership. It was always the rank and file members who seemed to be the responsible parties.

The suggestion was that something was lacking in the young Mason, and he needed to "wake up" and then give his total support to whatever was offered.

Was there a lacking in him?

Freemasonry either failed this young man in almost every way possible, or there was a genuine flaw in him. Was there, before he joined, a misunderstanding on his part as to the actual nature of Freemasonry? Is Freemasonry merely a club of good men who engage in charitable work and friendly meetings, or is it an organization that educates and uplifts its members through moral instruction?

In several publications, the young man saw written: "Freemasonry is the world's oldest and largest fraternity. Its history and tradition date to antiquity. Its singular purpose is to make good men better."

Okay, that's clear. But what does it mean and how do we do it?

Since this quote was written in a Masonic education publication, maybe that should give us a clue. We should teach and instruct our candidates. There are countless books and articles written on Masonic education. We learn the importance of education and teaching in our very rituals. But apart from the ritual, do we actually *teach* Freemasonry, or is it only words to be spoken or read and not acted upon?

How many young men are lost to us simply because we fail to do what we say we will do?

William Lowe Bryan (the tenth president of Indiana University) is credited with writing: "Education is one of the few things a person is willing to pay for and not get." This is sometimes very true, and has been for a good number of years, regarding Freemasonry. It seems that the hole that was left when quality education ceased to take place in the lodges may have been replaced with added fellowship.

That's not a bad thing, but it's not the lifeblood of Freemasonry. Initiation and making good men "better" are our main reasons for existence.

The passing of time is unavoidable. Every year, our lodges hold elections for officers to lead them for the following year. The young men who came into the lodge but learned very little about Freemasonry are now in leadership positions. They are the leaders, but truthfully, many are not qualified.

To be fair, it's not really their fault. Given the speed at which many of them go through the chairs, it's no surprise they're inexperienced. They are where they are because someone tapped them on the shoulder and asked them if they would accept a position. They were just trying to be helpful.

Maybe the lodge felt that it had no one else to ask and had to take whoever it could get. Perhaps it was felt that to take anyone, even someone very inexperienced, was better than closing shop.

Where Masonic education once took place, discussions of lodge picnics or other lodge events are heard at the meetings. The time that was once spent by the Worshipful Master on the planning of the Masonic education of the members is often now spent on trying to learn the very basics of lodge leadership.

Lodge meetings are only as long as felt necessary, and then the "enjoyable" time of the lodge takes place — sharing a few laughs with friends. The leaders are expected to keep the members happy, not spend too much money, and get through their year with as little hassle as possible. The "hole" was filled, and we are marking time, just getting through the years.

But marking time and just getting by does not secure the future of Freemasonry. It is not responsible. It is not enough that we *say* that we are "Freemasonry," but act like a club. We must either be what we say or admit to being something else.

To all the junior officers of Freemasonry, no matter if you are brand new to Freemasonry, or have been a Mason for a number of years and are only now returning to lodge activity, no matter what level of experience and knowledge you have, *stop*. Take a breath. You are not alone. You don't have to have a situation where young men are leaving your lodges because of claims that you are not giving them what they expected. You don't have to worry that you will, all of a sudden, be in charge and not know what in the world to do or say. You have Brothers who wish to help you.

Just as each of you had to step up and ask to join Freemasonry, you must now step up and make your needs and desires known. And when you are a junior officer is the time when you should do this.

The internet is filled with Masonic education websites, but which are reliable? You may wish to seek out the recognized and respected Masonic education sources. In the U.S., quality Masonic educational/service societies, which you can, and should, join, are designed to provide quality Masonic educational resources and services. Ask your Grand Lodge which organizations are recommended.

I believe deeply in the importance of finding balance in everything. Going too far one way or the other never seems to bring about what is truly desired. But what do we do about our present situation? We have already gone too far. Our lodges have taken on more of the appearance of clubs than lodges of moral instruction.

It was not done through maliciousness; it was done out of a desire to help and preserve. It did not happen all at once, but over a period of time. It was done with no ill intentions. We all know that there is a problem in our lodges. We know that they are not the same lodges as before.

We hear the stories of days long gone. Our leaders desire to do good, but some are uncertain as to which path is the best one. No one wishes for everything to fall apart on their watch. Some may feel that to do nothing is better than to do the wrong thing.

But cancer is never cured by inaction. There is an old Rosicrucian thought that everything felt to be of value must face the test of death. What is truly of value will come back alive. What is of no value will fade away.

Is Freemasonry of value?

I do not believe that society (or any group of people) is changed en masse by outside influences. I believe that change always comes through individual change. When we change as individuals, and if others change in a like manner, then society changes. I believe that the very first step we can take is to recognize that we are in trouble and traveling in the wrong direction.

Value is a perception. We place whatever value we choose on something. Value can also change. If you don't treat something as if it is special or valuable, it's not.

Anyone who knows me personally knows that I live in blue jeans. But those who only know me from lodge believe that I live in business suits. Going to lodge is something very special to me. I dress accordingly. If I didn't own a suit, I would clean myself and then put on the best shirt and slacks I owned.

Try this the next time you visit your lodge: act as if it is a *very* special occasion; as if you are going to a *very* special place to do *very* special things. Do what you would do if you were going to such a special event.

Always treat going to the lodge as something *very* important and special. Make that one permanent change in your life. Freemasonry will be what its members make it. The true and sole power within Freemasonry has always resided with its members — with you.

Thank you for buying this Cornerstone book!

For over 30 years now, we've tried to provide quality books on Masonic education, esoteric subjects, and general interest.Your support means everything to us and keeps us afloat. Cornerstone is by no means a large company. We are a small family-owned operation that depends on your support.

Please visit our website and have a look at the many books we offer as well as the different categories of books.

If your lodge, Grand Lodge, research lodge, book club, or other body would like to have quality Cornerstone books to sell or distribute, write us. We can give you outstanding books, prices, and service.

Thanks again!

Cornerstone Book Publishers
1cornerstonebooks@gmail.com
http://cornerstonepublishers.com

More Masonic Books from Cornerstone

Living Freemasonry
A Better Path to Travel
by Michael R. Poll
6x9 Softcover 180 pages
ISBN 99781934935958

The Particular Nature of Freemasons
by Michael R. Poll
6x9 Softcover 156 pages
ISBN 9781613423462

10,000 Famous Freemasons
4 Vol. Softcover Edition
by William Denslow
Foreword by Harry S. Truman
Cornerstone Foreword by Michael R. Poll
8.5 x 11, Softcover 2 Volumes 1,515 pages
ISBN 1887560319

Historical Inquiry into the Origins of the Ancient and Accepted Scottish Rite
by James Foulhouze
Edited by Jonathan K. Poll
Foreword by Michael R. Poll
6×9 Softcover 288 pages
ISBN: 978-1-61342-026-3

In His Own (w)Rite
by Michael R. Poll
6×9 Softcover 176 pages
ISBN: 1613421575

Cornerstone Book Publishers
www.cornerstonepublishers.com

More Masonic Books from Cornerstone

The Scottish Rite Papers
*A Study of the Troubled History of the Louisiana and
US Scottish Rite in the Early to Mid-1800s*
by Michael R. Poll
6x9 Softcover 240 pages
ISBN 9781613423448

Seeking Light
The Esoteric Heart of Freemasonry
by Michael R. Poll
6×9 Softcover 156 pages
ISBN: 1613422571

Measured Expectations
The Challenges of Today's Freemasonry
by Michael R. Poll
6×9 Softcover 180 pages
ISBN: 978-1613422946

A Masonic Evolution
The New World of Freemasonry
by Michael R. Poll
6×9 Softcover 176 pages
ISBN: 978-1-61342-315-8

Robert's Rules of Order: Masonic Edition
Revised by Michael R. Poll
6 x 9 Softcover 212 pages
ISBN 1887560076

Cornerstone Book Publishers
www.cornerstonepublishers.com

More Masonic Books from Cornerstone

An Encyclopedia of Freemasonry
by Albert Mackey
Revised by William J. Hughan and Edward L. Hawkins
Foreword by Michael R. Poll
8.5 x 11, Softcover 2 Volumes 960 pages
ISBN 1613422520

Masonic Enlightenment
The Philosophy, History and Wisdom of Freemasonry
Edited by Michael R. Poll
6 x 9 Softcover 180 pages
ISBN 1887560750

The Bonseigneur Rituals
A Rare Collection of 18th Century New Orleans Ecossais Rituals
Edited by Gerry L. Prinsen
Foreword by Michael R. Poll
8x10 Softcover 2 volumes 574 pages
ISBN 1934935344

Our Stations and Places - Masonic Officer's Handbook
by Henry G. Meacham
Revised by Michael R. Poll
6 x 9 Softcover 164 pages
ISBN: 1887560637

Knights & Freemasons: The Birth of Modern Freemasonry
By Albert Pike & Albert Mackey
Edited by Michael R. Poll
Foreword by S. Brent Morris
6 x 9 Softcover 178 pages
ISBN 1887560661

Cornerstone Book Publishers
www.cornerstonepublishers.com

New Orleans Scottish Rite College

www.youtube.com/c/NewOrleansScottishRiteCollege

Clear, Easy to Watch
Scottish Rite and Craft Lodge
Video Education

CORNERSTONE
BOOK PUBLISHERS

Outstanding Books • Outstanding Prices
Outstanding Service
One Stop for Masonic Education
Great Discounts on Bulk Orders

Visit Us Today!
www.cornerstonepublishers.com

Masonic, Scottish Rite, Esoteric &
Metaphysical Books
Masonic degree Charts & Art
Masonic Gifts

www.ingramcontent.com/pod-product-compliance
Lightning Source LLC
Chambersburg PA
CBHW021101090426
42738CB00006B/452

* 9 7 8 1 6 1 3 4 2 4 5 7 5 *